Notting Hill Editions is an independent British publisher. The company was founded by Tom Kremer (1930–2017), champion of innovation and the man responsible for popularising the Rubik's Cube.

After a successful business career in toy invention Tom decided, at the age of eighty, to fulfil his passion for literature. In a fast-moving digital world Tom's aim was to revive the art of the essay, and to create exceptionally beautiful books that would be lingered over and cherished.

Hailed as 'the shape of things to come', the family-run press brings to print the most surprising thinkers of past and present. In an era of information-overload, these collectible pocket-size books distil ideas that linger in the mind.

Xandra Bingley rode and trained ponies before she started work at the age of seventeen for MI5. She then worked for the *Atlantic Monthly Review* in Boston and the Kennedy Institute of Politics at Harvard. Subsequently in London she became a publisher's reader and then a commissioning editor at Jonathan Cape before she started her own literary agency. Her childhood wartime memoir *Bertie, May and Mrs Fish* was published to great acclaim in 2005. She lives in London.

Margaret Atwood is the author of more than fifty books of fiction, poetry, critical essays, and comics. Her work has been published in more than forty-five countries. Her latest novel, *The Testaments*, was a co-winner of the 2019 Booker Prize. Her other works of fiction include *Cat's Eye*, finalist for the 1989 Booker Prize; *Alias Grace*, which won the Giller Prize in Canada and the Premio Mondello in Italy; *The Blind Assassin*, winner of the 2000 Booker Prize; *The MaddAddam Trilogy*; and *Hag-Seed*. She is the recipient of numerous awards, including the Peace Prize of the German Book Trade, the Franz Kafka International Literary Prize, the PEN Center USA Lifetime Achievement Award, and the *Los Angeles Times* Innovator's Award. Her most recent book is *The Book of Lives: A Memoir of Sorts*. She lives in Toronto.

WAYS OF TELLING

—

Xandra Bingley

Introduced by
Margaret Atwood

Notting Hill Editions

Published in 2026
by Notting Hill Editions Ltd
Mirefoot, Burneside, Kendal LA8 9AB

EU Authorised Representative:
Easy Access System Europe
Mustamäe tee 50, 10621 Tallinn, Estonia
easproject.com
gpsr.requests@easproject.com

Cover design by Matthew Burne
Typeset by CB Editions, London
Printed and bound in the UK by Clays Ltd, Elcograf S.p.A.

A CIP record for this book is available from the British Library

ISBN 978-1-912559-89-3

nottinghilleditions.com

For Charlotte Nimmo & Brer Ruthven

'One should be light as a bird, and not like a feather.'

Paul Valery

'Can I be everyone else?'

A child

Contents

Introduction ix
The Writer 1
Down the Lane 4
Tree Boys 9
Bill Martin 13
No One Knows How Important I Am 24
American Soul 29
Herself 33
Lester 37
What the Children Like to Do 39
The Farm 41
Trains and Buses 44
Hero 49
Outside 52
After the Pop Concert 54
Cigarettes 58
A Fall 60
Hospital Notebook 65
Stay Alive 74
A Famous Man 79

Mouthing 86

The Punks Then 93

Christmas in the Shires 99

Vienna 103

Stow Fair 108

Princess Diana's Funeral 112

C.R.A.F.T. 133

Acknowledgements 134

MARGARET ATWOOD

– Introduction –

'O for a Life of Sensations rather than of Thoughts'
– John Keats

Ways of Telling isn't like any other book. Is it social reportage, the eye at the keyhole, the ear at the door? Is it a cross between Ivy Compton-Burnett, who wrote novels entirely composed of conversations, and Molly Bloom's soliloquy at the end of Joyce's *Ulysses*? Is it a study in textures and tones – the ripples on the pool of Being? Is it a collection of stones picked up at the beach – present, cherished, mute? Is it a variation of an exercise I used to give my writing students back when I had some: sit in a bus station, eavesdrop, and write down everything people say to each other? *Ways of Telling* is all this, and not this at all. It is its own thing.

No wonder, because Xandra Bingley is also her own thing. I first met her in 1983, when Graeme Gibson and I wanted to take a writing year in England in a key birding spot. But where? We decided on the north coast of Norfolk, where there were mud flats, marshes, and birds blown over the North Sea straight from Siberia.

Fine, but how to find a house to rent? Liz Calder, my editor at Jonathan Cape, said, 'Ask Xandra, she knows everything. Also she has a vicarage in Norfolk.' Xandra was a reader for Cape, meaning she read incoming manuscripts and advised about them – like one of the monologuists in

Ways of Telling. She had what art dealers might call 'a good eye', translated in the book world as 'a good ear'. We did ask Xandra, and she invited us to stay at the vicarage in Norfolk, and helped us find a place – another vicarage in Norfolk. It was there that I made some notes for *The Handmaid's Tale.* She also helped me source a used typewriter, which had a jamming L – giving me sentences like 'I ove you ots and ots,' which might have come straight out of Xandra's book.

Xandra was the closest thing to Mary Poppins I will ever meet – the film, not the books – very roll-up-your-sleeves practical and resourceful, and kind and helpful, but with a touch of – I won't call it wackiness. Let's say magic. She was also trained by MI5, and was sometimes known to say, 'I can kill with my thumbs.' It's an odd combo – an obsession with reading and words, plus the ability to pull rabbits or some sort of animal out of hats, plus an assassin's ability to cut to the bone – to which we can add a Dickensian interest in how ordinary people actually talk. Talk so often implies rather than stating, and evades rather than confronting. But we all read between the lines, and so will you as you encounter this book. Why don't we say what we mean? How do we say what we do mean? Is God in the details? How about the unspoken details?

Xandra Bingley has enriched my life, and the lives of so many people who have known her. Now she is about to enrich yours, in this curious and intriguing collection. Maybe we'll all learn to listen better. Or just listen.

– The Writer –

The writer steps up on a little stage in a big hall. Rows of chairs. An abstract mural various blues yellows small orange green white dashes. The writer sits down. A mic is clipped on his jacket lapel his not a loud tweed just pale brown and another brown. He reads to us from his new novel. He reads. And he reads. And he reads more. He reads on and on. We the audience look content. Perhaps we turn back into children. Being read to at bedtime. We relax. Start to feel drowsy. Just a little bit drowsy. Today is getting forgotten. Someone is doing something for us. The writer. He reads on and on. Just reading a story out loud. A nice thing to happen. That's what we come for. And the writer is reading and reading. His story goes on and on it's nice listening.

Then the organiser jumps up on the small stage says to the writer and we hear what the organiser says because he leans down to speak to the writer mouth close to the mic on the writer's tweed jacket lapel. The organiser arranged the reading sold the tickets put chairs in rows poured out glasses of red and white wine at the hall entrance paid for the hire of the hall and he says to the writer we are here for a limited time so it would be good to leave enough time for audience questions.

The writer says I'd like to read for a bit longer I haven't read this novel out loud before I'm really enjoying reading.

So the organiser says of course we have the hall for half an hour more and there's book signing to fit in to the time and jumps off the small stage and sits down.

The writer reads on. He reads on so long that the organiser jumps up again to say pretty much the same thing we all hear because of the mic on the writer's tweed jacket lapel and the only real difference is that the organiser sounds more urgent and says less because he knows that the writer knows what it is he is going to say and is saying because he has said the words once already.

The writer reads on. And on. And we are dozing. Children at bedtime being read a story. Children being read to sleep. Children being read towards the start of another day. Another adventure. Good or bad. Then suddenly the writer stops reading. The organiser jumps up on the small stage. He says thank you to the writer and looks at the audience and says we have just a short time for questions and then the writer will kindly sign copies of his books. Any questions?

The audience is silent. I sit at the back of the hall. I know how to fill an awkward moment with words. And to notice when an awkward moment is happening. I know how to be helpful. So I hold up my hand just to make something happen. To set the ball rolling. To wake up the audience. I have nothing particular to ask. That is not the point of my hand going up. The organiser points at me over the heads of the audience and says yes? And I say to the writer why do you enjoy reading aloud so much? And the writer says because I was read to at bedtime as a child by my parents and I always enjoyed hearing a story before going to sleep at night. And then the writer stops and looks at us and says that is not true. I was never read to as a child. My father now and then read *Rudolph the Red-Nosed Reindeer* to me. And I stand up at the back of the audience and say but that is a Christmas song. And the writer says I know but occasionally my father read *Rudolph the Red-Nosed Reindeer* out loud to me. Then the organiser says I'm afraid that is all the questions we have time for. Anyone who would like their book signed by the writer come up here please.

So what has happened? Was it that we saw a writer in a magic moment of creativity? The thing that usually happens when a writer is alone. A writer alone in his room. I think so.

Afterwards in the pub a couple at the next table are staring at me as I write this. So I'm stopping now. The man says please excuse us for watching you. Do tell us what are you writing?

– Down the Lane –

Down the lane there is no one and in my mouth the sweet seaside taste of bananas and my green car black wheels parked on jagged spring nettles rust spotted dock leaves lavender nettle mouths torn thistle swords and in the car is my mother's ashes inside a nice pine box and on the box lid a brass rectangle and on the brass is her maiden name and her married name and the years she lived AD and she and I and the dog are on the way to a churchyard beside the church where she knelt and prayed and stood and sang and sat and listened and for sure there wasn't ever a day when her dog her daughter her god weren't in her thoughts.

I sit in the sunshine warm as toast shoulders on hay bales piled up in a barn. The dog has left me. A split flock of pigeons fly overhead fast and low tunes air to music blackbirds thrushes bees a small plane engine a breeze in dock leaves a blue and rusty harrow chain swings clicks black plastic rags flap and hair wisps blow all across my eyes all sounds my dead mother heard and loved and the gorgeous baked green to gold grey hay scent on a breeze passes by.

The dog is lost not here near me and my sudden fear is because animals come first she said never ever leave an animal behind. Leave dog here. I can't leave dog. Her ash her soul her in memory will not lie peaceful and still will shift and wrinkle and lump and stir no her ashes must lie stiller than the soil I pray and now I hear stick breaks a dog broken stick I whistle two notes high low same as she whistled a red admiral butterfly dithers past my toes then flies away a wasp zigzags up and down above my arm a travelling breeze comes up the green blackthorn hedge in and out of ivy crawling along black oak branches into and out of my hair and flaps black plastic on barbed wire strands.

I see cold breezes travel on up the hedge and I am anxious about time and the dog and the years until I die and my breath halts and jumps and I hear her say this way darling follow me it won't take long now and tears trickle from my eyes onto my hand onto plastic pen and my mother and I are close again and I breathe deep to whistle and dog is through the hedge in front of me taking no notice of me at all and I stop my writing and smile and say out loud thanks mum.

In her village churchyard the dog and I sit on grass beside a turf cut out so the earth is open ready waiting for her ashes. The golden dog pants slah-slah-slah. Yellow aconites violets blue speedwell white cherry blossoms shiver and across a grey yellow stone lichen mossy wall a scattered flock of sheep and by the vicarage wall yellow daffs white narcissi buttermilk primroses bumblebees and scythed dry grass and up the church tower three sharp toothy gargoyles stare big stone eyes clutch parapets their stone chins on their stone arms waiting for rain to dribble spout from their stone grins.

The vicar stands in sunshine in his full-length ironed white cassock and holds the book and says the prayers dust to dust and so on and His ever-loving arms and eternal faith and for our Lord Jesus Christ sake in whose care and so on. I stand holding her box of ashes thinking war love war love war so long nineteen hundred and thirteen her birth is ago before cars radios television planes fertilizers atomic bombs steel hulls reinforced concrete drip dry non crease psychiatry road rage hot power showers how strong tough my gentle mother had to be to keep to her true self and how here in sunshine stood among flowers pigeons lambs birds dog I know I was a cruel mean daughter and also a loving one and how despicable cruelty is and whether it begins in war I don't know but sure as eggs is eggs she lived through war I hear clip clop clip clop two ridden horses trot up the farm lane and my parents talking in peacetime before I knew them.

Inside the church a small red candle flame in a gold candlestick burns as a pedal organ growls puffs whines along cosy sad songs and I sing cold air into my lips and the dog cries his chin on the toe of my silver leather boot on a kneeler in a wooden pew and I hold out prayerful hands for jammy vinegar taste of wine and melting penny white wafer bread the body of Christ the Blood of Christ so don't let anyone suffer for me no alleluia repent our great high priest oh thou on earth both priest and victim so the offertory hymn begins and a lady with a velvet money-bag walks nearer I scrubble in midnight blue velvet pocket for pounds and out come things off the early morning hill three fine pheasant feathers marked by camouflage light grey white specks and after I drop a coin in her collection bag and put my three feathers on the pew and count first feather twenty-two tiny dashes on moths wings and on second feather ten white light flashes and ten brown grey bridges wide at tips and on third feather twelve white rockets in grey brown sky dark one quarter at cloudy ice tips to spider web quill ends. Also in my pocket is a gun cartridge lemon primrose cardboard fits flush into rusted brass end engraved 70mm Winchester 71/2 barrel eaten halfway from brass to spent gunshot end all chewed squashed flat ripped torn broken by teeth or by fire I don't know any more I would've when but not now I'm not a country woman.

I remember once I telephone my mother hear her voice odd sad a little choked her breath held down tight quick shallow and I say what's happened are you all right how is Ben he is her elderly American lover and she says I don't know he's been cooking fish in garlic all morning it smells I can't stand it I threw it out of the window he's gone out I don't know where do you think he'll come back and I say yes he will be back and think that greedy sentimental scrounger her doubts are born in his lack of love for her and I say he's up the road in the pub I bet he's there you go and see. Now that pub is where I am the pub where I wasn't allowed inside these are the men red faced and proud and away to the side sat further on back used to be the women.

That night I hear lambs bleat in the dark a sad cry a thumb run along comb teeth fast and dog ruffwruffs at a boy and girl outside my window in love and I lie and listen to blackbird whistle then up and out dog and I go along the early green valley and angry rooks furious wings clap clap a hurricane as killer dog and I pass by and pheasants shout go back go back. Nonetheless dog and I head uphill to sun we pass dark woodside and rabbits beetles mice small unseen things halt listen run hide and I call good dog come and click on his lead so up we go between steep green prickly white flower blackthorns past washed pink wild roses and gorse yoke yellow flower shells till my uphillside dog pulls my arm my feet prance on lemony cowslips I stand still and listen. No lambs no pheasant chicks none so I let dog run I lay my midnight blue coat down on grass shiny blue in this early misty morning and lean back shoulders on a silver lichen flat grey stonewall that runs horizons for miles.

In half an hour the rooks quiet down and dog shoves under brambles a lark song ripples at my eye level past the hillside rim and I hear pony hoofbeats across the valley and a hare lollollops stop lollollop stop downhill in slalom lines all haunches his ears flat down and dog snuffs hare scent dog stretches out twice his usual length dog dashes down steep hillside I stand I see golden dog hit green valley floor roll stand haul up far hill and hare and dog gold disappear in blackthorns shade and close by me two emeralds flash greenfinches or lost parrots who knows then a white feather floats past the other way and again hoofbeat sounds down below and flowering May a snow white star shaped copse and I am nearly cold till dog comes back his long black flap tongue sprays grass he shakes fur dry lies stares at hare gone hill.

– Tree Boys –

Out in the street tree surgeon boys throw up pulley ropes on grapple hooks tighten buckles on wide-webbed belts lean back to march up trees kick heels off tree trunks. Orange electric saws hang off belts and switched on scream. The boys fly sideways in green leaves. Boys come from different countries. Not all speak English. Talking is not what they are paid to do. Trimmers away of dark. Choreographers of light. Aviators. They know metamorphosis. They think differently to us. Anyone can see that. I say what's it like up there? It's fantastic it's hard to describe I can't live without it. I've tried. After I got married. I did postal work. I couldn't keep to it. I missed the height. I ask is it ever frightening? Yeah sometimes. I say have any of you fallen? Broke a leg my first time. Never since. I ask why's it good up there? Well you find that out when you come down.

I say do you go out? D'you drink and dance? Everything. Mostly women. And drink. Mostly women though. Up all night can't sleep sometimes. I'm still up there aren't I? Can't get myself down. Makes it hard to settle. Hard to stay home. You want to keep on. I ask are you all married? Sort of. That is you can't have it both ways. Up there and stay home. I see a broken heart story coming. A girl crying why're you always forever up in trees for god's sake.

In the street tree roots crack pavement slabs wriggle

under garden walls root hairs creep towards light. My neighbour wants a tree cut down. He's deaf and shouts. Inside my house I hear him shouting at his wife. He stands yells at a tree boy cut off those bloody branches cut the whole bloody tree bloody down. He says loudly sod the Council and walks away indoors. I stand still.

Neighbour Man's wife cooks washes up his meals day after week after year. Sixty something years. A teenage bride. She starts into senility in her seventies. Neighbour Man looks tired out in the street. He snaps if I say how are you? One day I say I haven't seen your wife outdoors is she well? Neighbour Man says nowadays she wakes me up every bloody night. She tells me get up you get your clothes on get me roast chicken and roast potatoes and peas and Bisto gravy I'm famished. I say can't you ask her go off back to sleep now and we'll have roast chicken tomorrow. He mumbles I bloody do she gets bloody angry she throws things at me you know. I'd stay in bed asleep if she'd stop chucking jugs of damned cold water over me. I've been up cooking for her every bloody night every day this bloody week.

I think how very amazing his wife has made him learn to cook clever tiny wifey after all these years all that servant behaviour. Now I see her at a window and she looks fine on it. Small smiley white hair she dies soon. Neighbour Man looks rested again. He says good thing I learned to cook I don't bloody enjoy it mind.

Neighbour Man takes his Chow dog promenading in the park first thing. I hear him call Mandy Mandy come along my darling come on darling this way sweetheart that's far enough Mandy girl now back home we go. He feeds Mandy dog cupcakes shortbread biscuits raw mince rice pudding cream. Mandy dog pants waddles slower slower. Mandy dog dies sooner than she ought. Neighbour Man grieves for a week. Gets a new Mandy dog same colour same shape same breed same name. I hear him call again Mandy come along my darling come on darling this way sweetheart that's far enough Mandy girl now back home we go. He feeds second Mandy dog cupcakes shortbread biscuits raw mince rice pudding cream. Mandy dog pants waddles slower slower. Second Mandy dog dies sooner than she ought. Neighbour Man grieves for a week. Then off he goes. Buys third Mandy dog. Same words.

Two little girls say to Neighbour Man your dog's fat is it going to die can we watch please please we want to see. One day the little girls put on their coats and say we're going to tell Neighbour Man his Mandy dog is dead. I say how do you know? The girls chant it's in his garden dead. I look out of the window and see Mandy dog asleep on the grass. The sash window rattles up. The dog sits up. The little girls say we're going to tell him anyway. Up Neighbour Man's front steps go two little girls. Ring his doorbell. Neighbour Man opens the door. The girls chant your dog is dead your dog is dead we've come to tell you we've come to tell you. Mandy dog waddles to the door. The little girls chant we came to tell you we're going home now goodbye goodbye.

Neighbour Man says to me I'll be dead soon if something's not done about that bloody tree just you look at the crack in that wall this house is falling down around me I want my hundredth birthday telegram from the Queen that's what I bloody want.

I drive to the Greek-Cypriot garage. I ask if they sell car radio aerials? A mechanic grins. He says shake my hand. I near as nothing clasp his oily hand with my clean sunburnt one. I laugh say you're all so bad in here. The two mechanics roll their eyes. Yes one says but an aerial is expensive. Your car is foreign so we have to send away. I say isn't there a cheap aerial I don't listen to my car radio very often. He stares at patterns of pigeon shit on my car roof and the limp radio aerial. He says I don't know. His voice is mellow. I dream of abroad. A hot wandering holiday driving a well-preserved Citroën car. He says do you know what? Do we have coat hangers? He disappears among cars hoisted up to fly with silent engines at the back of the shed. When he comes back he is twisting a wire coat hanger. He says what would you like?

I remember a friend whose car aerial is a wire coat hanger duck. I say a duck please. Then I remember my friend is an artist. A wire beak and wire small duck head could easily go wrong in a mechanic's big oily hands. I'd be stuck with a deformed duck for years out of gratitude. I say no a star. A star thank you. I meant to say a tree. Perhaps I did say tree. I am trying to think about trees a lot of the time now for a work project that is good but slow. The big oily hands mechanic has decided on a star. He says quietly she wants a tree she wants a tree as he bends wire into a star. He wrenches the old aerial off and sticks on my wire star. Wonderful I say. I think maybe an aerial star will make me a star. Look I say to Andreos the garage owner as he comes in. You'll be a star now he says. I drive home switching radio stations all the way and think I am a foolish woman not to have made my own star.

– Bill Martin –

A breeze blows autumn leaves around The Old Forge. Bill Martin looks in the door.

Bill Martin is eighty-six and a handsome man. In a war-time photograph he is tall lean and smiling stood under a tree in army uniform. He holds a motorbike fondly one hand on the handlebar one hand on the seat. Same as I'd hold a pony that I loved.

Bill Martin and I are happy together. He is deaf so there is no point in my talking to him all the time. I am quieter with him and I write more. He is putting a lock on the old forge door so no one can break in on me if I sit in candlelight at night to write. His bony face turns my way. He says what tickles me is this whacking great bolt you got to keep out marauders comes with these incy wincey little teeny weeny screws. I know I say. But I don't know. I'd never have noticed how small the screws are if he hadn't said. If I hadn't been with him I'd never have cried down at the council dump as I threw out my mother's possessions after she's died. And I wouldn't have dressed up in a flowery summer straw hat and my prettiest dress to go down to the dump. Or gone on afterwards to the café where we have tea and watch water rush across Dobbs Weir. I push the forge door full open to let in the autumn sun. He turns away to pick up a screwdriver then turns around and says how did that door get there you moved the door didn't you you shouldn't have done that.

Then he says I suppose the loneliest time in the war was in the desert. I was a dispatch rider. The chain broke on my motorbike somewhere in Africa miles from nowhere. That was lonely. But my luck held. I found the thing I needed in my toolkit box. Bill Martin smiles at me. His brown flecked eyes magnified behind dirty thick glass lenses.

Were you out in the desert at night on your own.

Oh lord no. It was day. Thank heavens.

Did your bike ever break down at night in the desert.

No never sent out at night always day. Told go in that direction until you see a burnt out tank. Then turn left or right keep on going. Look for a burnt out gun or whatever it was. Never got lost not once.

Was it written down.

Not likely.

How far did you go.

I don't know for miles.

You must have a good memory.

Not any more. I never took my leave. I stayed on duty when the others went into towns on the coast. I never wanted to. You can keep your popsies in the towns was what I thought.

His big hands are brown. He holds up the screwdriver above his head and shoves it horizontally at the screw. He turns one half circle and thrusts and turns another half circle and thrusts again and again. I sit behind him at my table and watch his shoulders shift and the backs of his knees hollow and straighten and the rhythms in his body.

Bill Martin flew to Texas to his daughter's wedding. His only time in a plane. He went with Grace his wife. He bought four things for the journey. Two shirts a pair of shoes a second pair of spectacles a torch. After telling me he says I miss Grace.

I say I know.

But I don't know. I only know about a very long marriage because he has told me. They got married when he was twenty-two. Grace died six years ago when he was seventy-four. That's fifty-two years. Eighteen thousand nine hundred and eighty nights together except for in the war.

He says I don't know how you can stand that noise while you're working.

I say that's Mozart.

He says Mozart cor phew was that the noise he made while he was dying what a melancholy howl.

He says you should get a curtain over that door for the draughts a curtain that's a tight fit. You should say it like this *ttightt-fitt-ttightt-fitt.* Not like you do. And he slackens his mouth and mimics me. *Iye-lit.* That's what you say.

My dog barks at the sheep in the field outside. I call Sam Sam don't tease the sheep. Bill Martin says does he understand.

I say yes if I pronounce the t's clearly.

He looks at me as if I am stupid and he says how many t's in sheep.

I say I said *sheet* not sheep so the dog would understand.

Now we look at each other as if we've won a prize. A phonetic joke shared with a deaf person is a rare thing.

He says I wonder if the first girl I walked down that hill

with is still alive. He points the screwdriver at the forge door.

I say what.

He says I wonder if the first girl I walked through The Pollards with is still alive she was a bit older than me and the fellow she was with is dead and here's me still buggering about incredible isn't it.

He hates being deaf and his deafness annoys me when we talk. He is fearful that if he asks his doctor for a hearing aid he might lose his driving license. He is a dangerous driver dashing over crossroads as if he is still in the desert.

Bill Martin says nine o'clock tomorrow I'll be at Stansted Airport.

Why.

To take a girl to catch a plane. Emily Allen who makes lovely trifles which she has not made me one for a long while. I'm very lucky to be here. Lucky to be alive.

We're very lucky you're here don't you know that.

No.

My mother told you that didn't she.

He screws up his face raises his eyes says nooww pronounced like through.

He says I reckon that tree down there where I carved my name has died. They're easy to write on the beeches.

Yes and walnuts.

I don't know if walnuts do have a soft bark you can write on. On a walnut tree on our farm was carved Mick loves Mary inside a heart and I stood looking on tiptoe thinking love that will happen to me my name will be somewhere on a tree.

Bill Martin says to Sam the dog you've got long eyelashes

why've you got such long eyelashes to keep the sun out of your eyes I reckon and you've been putting your eyes in the sun you mustn't do that you'll be blinking all night.

I am typing all the time and he says I don't know how your brain can work that quick and I say nor do I it probably doesn't it's probably nonsense I'm writing I'll read it to you when it's done.

He says how d'you begin . . . once upon a time.

Sort of.

He says I make up stories when I'm trying to get to sleep at night. He smiles shyly.

What stories d'you make up.

I'm in Walthamstow and there's this poor old lady walking along with a lot of shopping and she puts it down and I ask her if she'd like me to carry it for her and if she says yes and I take it for her and we get on the bus and I ask her if she'd like to come to the café and have a biscuit and a cup of tea and if she says yes we sit in the café and then my other friend Emily is there the one I'm taking to Stanstead Airport in the morning and we sit and chat and then the first one with the bags gets up to go off to see her friend and I say to her if your friend by chance hasn't got room for you to stay and you decide to stay I do have a spare room at my place and then I go back to talking to Emily and then maybe Edna my other friend comes into the café and so it goes on one thing leads to another it all mounts up and keeps on going.

I am smiling because it's a story and I love stories.

In the afternoon Bill Martin leaves and I am bereft. I write no more until tomorrow. Many times in the night the dog barks and a sheep coughs.

Sshhh Sam I say the sheep's all right but the sheep isn't. The sheep is dying and the dog barks a low harsh anger.

Bill Martin thinks about Grace every day and he says in the nights he reaches out his hand to touch her.

He tells me the first girl I took out I found out she was showing my love letters to her girl friends so when I found out I cut her dead whenever I saw her after that.

I say oh that must have hurt so much and my voice comes out low in a down curve sound.

Silence. I think of him. I see a teenage boy. A boy like in a Joseph Wright of Derby painting half in the dark not knowing what would follow not seeing clearly.

I say how old were you.

Fifteen.

I think fifteen. Fifteen. Writing love letters sixty-five years ago. What did he wear. Where did he sit. What was his pen. What paper. What did he see when he looked up. I am too late. I am afraid I am too late. Sixty-five years. Bill Martin please remember and tell me what you wrote. Or else I have to remember for myself.

He says what's that stuff.

He is looking across the forge at me. I've taken out a black cardboard box of tea from a polished walnut tea caddy I've brought from my mother's house. The caddy has a silver tin lining and Raj Tea Company, Bangalore, India stamped on the front.

It's not the Earl Grey tea you don't like. Look.

No thanks.

It's English Breakfast Tea it's quite good.

I like Tetley's tea.

Once in a Chinese restaurant . . .

In a what.

I make him a mug of Tetley tea and one of Earl Grey tea for myself. I'd like to tell him about the Chinese restaurant the evening I sip tea from a china cup with no handle and I say to my man this is delicious why on earth d'you drink that Tetley's it's probably leftover tea leaves swept up off the tea factory floor and I beckon to a waiter imperiously and I ask what is the name of your deliciously aromatic tea and the waiter grins broadly and says Tetlee-teabag-tea and I feel dislike of myself and embarrassment in equal parts.

I give the mug of Tetleys to Bill Martin and say here you are.

He says thank you did you put three sugars in.

Yes I say and carefully place two Rich Tea sweet biscuits on his knee on the fawn corduroy material of his trousers and he says I thought I was going to have chocolate biscuits.

Not till we've finished these. I know they're not very nice.

They're not bad just dull.

I have inherited the Rich Tea biscuits from my mother and since she was the way she was and I am the way I am I can't throw them away so Bill Martin and Sam the dog and I are eating them. Tomorrow maybe I'll get some chocolate ones anyway.

Tomorrow I buy a packet of expensive German plump heart-shaped chocolated on one side biscuits before Bill Martin arrives back from his drive with Emily Alley to Stansted Airport. The biscuits feel soft as my mother's cheeks and arms. For years I couldn't touch my mother. Only quickly. She looked at me pleadingly like the dog does when he wants food. Her sorrowfulness and her belief in Jesus' suffering. Why doesn't he come. Bill Martin I don't want to remember all this. Bill Martin let's have your life not mine.

On Sundays when I am a child my mother drives country lanes to the village church in her midnight blue Ford V8 Pilot sedan. Roads my father drives a half hour earlier in his dove-grey convertible Daimler to the same church as my mother. On Saturdays before each Sunday I fret about which parent's car to go to church in. Which parent to choose. At a time like this when I'm back in my past I should not be alone. Where is he. Crashed. Hurt. Dead maybe. Died in his sleep maybe. I want to eat all the chocolate heart biscuits. I want loud music. And wine. Isn't that what wine and music are for. To shift our sorrows. Quickly write quickly. At church I wear pink lambswool twinset jerseys a pleated grey skirt seamed nylon stockings clipped to a white cotton and lace garter belt. Brown leather lace-up brogues punctured by swirls of holes.

Why doesn't he come. I keep on staring out of the forge window. Eating drinking. Listening to music. The past has to have good bits. Look how lovely the trees on the horizon are. Someone wrote surely of all the wonders of the world the horizon is the greatest.

Bill Martin comes into the forge and says have you lit it.

No.

He bends. Folds up. Like a man starting to have a stroke. Close to the wood burner. He scrumples newspaper from my log basket into the grate. I hear him mutter won't bloody light must be bloody damp. We kneel side by side. We stare at the flame. I put my hand on his shoulder. The flame is tiny and coloured lemon and pale blue. Flame squiggles along the white rim of paper not touching black print flame bites a rippled curve into the words and flares up yellow. We watch a few seconds more but it's over for us. Now we are interested in smoke. I see it first. A wave curls up heads for the door out towards the trees.

I stand up. Bill Martin doesn't move. Smoke comes pouring from around the edges of the wood burner closed doors. He opens the wood burner. Paper stops burning. He puts his big hands inside . . . slams iron back and forth . . . gasps . . . won't bloody come out . . . you should put a . . . chimney on your roof . . . you haven't got . . . enough . . . air.

The forge is all smoky. We go out. Stand side by side. Sheep cluster in the field like rocks in woollen mist. Bill Martin lifts his head to declaim to the rising smoke

> I see before me a gladiator lie
> He leans upon his hand
> His manly brow condensed with death
> Butchered to make a Roman holiday.

He says my teacher criticised the way I said that. Told me put more expression into it Martin. I didn't know what sort of expression he wanted. Swear words or what.

We sit in my dead mother's wicker chairs and look out at the trees starting to turn different autumn colours. I ask him do you miss her dog.

What he shouts.

Do you miss my mother's dog.

Oh yes I miss the dog I thought you said fog not dog

people slur their words together you do it you don't separate the words wonder where the dog is now.

I know where the dog is. A gamekeeper was asked to put the dog down. To kill the dog. The gamekeeper had been a prisoner of war in a Japanese concentration camp. He showed me his grey blanket from the camp. A four digit number sewn on in black stitches. I asked him how did you survive that terrible time. He said I stayed alive because I was small . . . anyone big died

Bill Martin says I miss her not her dog me going in for a cup of tea and sitting where I did by the window I'd knock things off the shelf sitting down. He smiles. His mouth makes a wide loop and I smile back because the look on his face rearranges things. My sorrow and her death. Like in wartime when small planes dropped strips of silver tinsel on our farmyard on barns stables cows geese hens and we laughed when that happened. That never happened in peacetime.

Bill Martin says Lascars used to wake us early before they started cleaning up.

Lascars . . .

L-A-S-C-A-R-S.

What are Lascars.

Foreign sailors black men wakee wakee cleanee deckee on the troop ship then you'd skiddaddle fast or they'd make your blanket sopping wet three weeks out of seven I was sick all the rubbish was kept aboard in the day to throw in the sea at night in case submarines found out what direction we were sailing in I stood all day beside the rubbish don't know what I looked like know what I smelt like don't know how long it took us to come home nine months maybe I had to go didn't I for king and country.

My mother and I went to Buckingham Palace to see my father get a war medal and we sat in a ballroom on chairs with gold legs and soldiers with swords in black and scarlet uniforms stood to attention near us. I'd never left our farm before except to go shopping in our village with our pony Merrylegs pulling a green cart. The king as everyone knew and pitied him for had a stammer. My father stammered if he felt nervous. I said afterwards daddy daddy you talked to the king for longer than anyone else did. My father said y-y-yes a-a-and n-n-neither of us s-s-said a w-w-w-word.

Animals get stuck too. Old Man's Beard catches the big curved horns of Beau Brummel our tall Ayreshire farm bull named after the famous Regency dandy. The bull slips the ring in his nose ring off the hook and pole he is led by and prances dances along the lane passing by wild cornflowers dog roses garlic till vines hanging off Alders halt him. Beau Brummel shakes his head frantically to try to escape. My father roars with laughter shouting no more damned ballroom dancing for you today old boy. My mother tells me the other name for Old Man's Beard is Traveller's Joy.

In winter at The Old Forge I and girls ten and eleven and Sam our dog drive to collect a green kitchen dresser I've bought in a junk shop. A snowstorm swirls across roads. The oak tree by the forge the girls the dog are snow white glamourous. Bill Martin screws hooks in the dresser for cups to hang on. Snowflakes sprinkle whiteness on our sleeping bodies lying in a row on rush matting. Girl ten has four children now. The green dresser is in her home. Bill Martin died.

– No One Knows How Important I Am –

No one a creepy crawly stands at the top of the stairs and kind of barks. Then I run. I laugh first. I plan to laugh fast. A quick smack-smack plan but in fact I run. I do laugh. A hyena-ish smirk I was going to say but when I hear myself I am a lamb. A little bleat and then I'm off running through canyons dressing rooms kitchens forests lines of tin cans I run past horses and dolls. Horses dressed as dolls. Dolls on all fours. Dolls with tails.

You know how it is when you're scared. It's a crazy thing. Nothing fits. The arms of my jersey are tight as fists. Not me. Not me I wail to myself. I'm not really running. I'm in bed at night. Night that is early morning. There's a lump beside me. A man.

I have a cry when he's asleep. Or I get up and eat white bread and spoon after spoon of strawberry jam. And I say to myself I'll stop soon. No more jam. Less bread. I'll leave. I'll live on my own. Then I won't be afraid.

Do I leave? No fear. That's an old saying. Can you come out to play? Climb the church tower with me or jump off a wall into the sea or lie by train tracks wait for a train? No fear. I stay because love is a scary thing. Everyone knows that. I'm just doing bits of it wrong.

Take Tuesday. He was so sweet. Came to get me at work. The girls in my office said lucky you you're a lucky one mine never picks me up from work. I beam at the girls and at him. My man looks serious. As if he only just has time to do this thing. By-ee-ee I say to the girls see you tomorrow. Off we speed in his car. Thanks for coming I say. How was your day. Then it begins. I can't hear a thing. Something's wrong. Why can't I hear?

I turn my head his way. I see his mouth move. He is mouthing words. His eyes look where they should be looking. Ahead at the windscreen. Through the windscreen. I see the strong bones of his chin. Strong muscles and bones. Shit-shit-shit I hear him say oh-fuck-off. A driver shoves up the inside lane gets to green lights ahead of my man.

I'm doing something wrong I'm thinking. I'll sit quietly. He's tired. He has a responsible job. People's money is in his hands. People's money is in my hands in my work. The money I get for them comes from things they love to create. They create stories. That's a big difference. I know that's how they wish to spend time. I don't think he likes to spend time the ways that he does. His work's all on paper. On screens. The people whose money he makes aren't there in the rooms where he is. I think that's hard. Not to be able to see what's going on. Not to hear the words thank you. Not to see a person smile at him or say I've waited for this for so long.

Remember the American pilot who flew the plane that dropped the Hiroshima bomb? Someone asked him what did it feel like to you when you dropped the bomb. The pilot replied I did what I set out to do. I went there and did it then I came back. I don't feel guilty. I had a job to do and I did it. Something like that. When I read what the pilot said I thought Jesus some mental editing must have gone on I mean he'd seen photos taken. The atomic mushroom cloud. People with skin hanging off faces and hands. It seems that being up in his plane didn't join up with pain he saw in photos. People's hands' burnt skin. His hands at the controls of his plane. Him flying the plane. Whatever people below were doing just then.

My man isn't cruel at work. Or maybe he is. I'm sure he isn't. And anyway aren't there laws to restrain cruelty in money manoeuvres. I don't expect that kind of law is foolproof. But laws create a restraining demand on behaviour unaccepting of agreed morality. That's all a bit long. Long words come to me more when I'm anxious.

I take a look at his jaw again. And his forehead. It's big. I love his forehead. All those brains. He'll know what to do. When we get home we'll be happy and talking again.

I'll sit quietly for now. It's not that I'm scared. Well I am. I do rate his possible car crash statistical odds quite high. It's the tension. I doubt he can feel the form of the thing called a car in his hands. It must be more like he's gripping onto his own knuckles and bones. The steering wheel turns when his muscles and bones must turn. That's different. Like in an accident.

I love the sensation of turning a wheel attached to wheels on the road. I love the slow and quick a car goes. How the back follows the front. At corners a press of my foot can tip the car angle as well as increase the speed. I love all that. It's like flying. Watching birds I get ideas about driving. It's silly I know. The car's on the road. The bird's in the air. Not completely silly. Birds wheel in the sky. It's a phrase. The car flew. Anyway today we're stuck in a jam. Maybe that's why I eat jam in the night. So there's no traffic jams. Eating up all the jams in town. So we'll fly home.

I'm sad now. Sad playing with words is not my man's fun. I'm sad and I'm guessing he's lonely again. I'll try thinking of words he likes hearing. They're so out of my reach. I'm thinking how can I earn money this instant to give him. Say to him I've got loads of money for you. Not true and anyway he wouldn't like to be given money by me. Is that because I'm a woman? If I rip off my dress so he sees me delicious beside him. That could be fun. Sadly fun just for fun hardly ever turns into money.

Suddenly he says how was your day.

I say it was fine I had one success and you know Joan who the new man in publicity fancies she's the one who came home to ours with me for a drink once well she was saying to me . . . this isn't interesting him so I say that's not very interesting now I think about it but there's something you'd like that's come in a new History of the World by a man called... I stop then. I must be tired. I know that to write a history of the world's what my man would himself like to have done. Do now. How could I forget that. He won't want to know a new world history's been done.

I think what else was going on today. I say someone brought this manuscript in and wouldn't go away. I heard Dinah at the front desk say it's no point telling me what's in your book. I don't like reading. The person kept saying Miss Byron? You are Miss Byron? The person can't believe Dinah's not interested with a name the same as Byron the poet.

Good for Dinah he says.

That's weird I think. Good for Dinah not to like reading? My man reads.

I read for a living. That's a bit weird. Maybe good for Dinah not to care about writers? So it's good to not care about writers? So it's bad to be me who does care about writers all day. I'm confused. Traffic's moving. We'll be home soon.

Soon soon we'll be home. The evening will hurry by. He'll sleep. I'll be awake. I'll watch the night sky. I'll get up and eat bread and jam. I'll write a story.

Tomorrow will come. I wonder how long will all this go on.

– American Soul –

James Brown Prince of Soul plays Boston Garden Arena. It's 1968. Racial segregation is legally over. Martin Luther King is shot dead the day before. In this city fighting happens over mixed race school bussing over everything. The first the only Boston Massachusetts USA white black anyone can get a rock-concert ticket tonight. Racial tension everywhere. Nearby Roxbury's black neighbourhood gets set on fire most nights. Here we are at last together at this sell-out whites take expensive seats up front of course plus of course in enormous Boston Garden two hundred three hundred four hundred Boston cops stand three deep. Blue uniform men ring round everyone so James Brown can sing and play for us we love this man.

James Brown's concert finale. Two acolytes place his lovely many coloured cloak across his shoulders beautiful James Brown swirls and swirls again his famous swirling brilliant blue green red silver gold for us all. He walks away upstage we scream shout for him to come back give us music rhythm soul we can't be without you not now not for evermore his power races in our hearts a musical cataract drowns us for two gorgeous hours now we're all standing shoving pushing forwards if we can closer to the stage nearer our prince he'll sing more songs to us his yes here he comes for us his cloak a many coloured cave we're so happy we dance sing clap sway all friends finally free to be then screams start up scared sounds screams shouts yells I'm hit I'm bad hurt faces arms ribs nightsticks long as a man's forearm cops carry on black gun belts a nightstick is a flat iron bar look see cops at work furiously fast why what's gone wrong nothing's wrong cops rushed to nightstick smack anyone everyone who's here for James Brown cops forget US Federal Law passed four years ago rules we can yes we may legally all be together at any time anywhere. Cops tear gas us all air stinks hurts we cry we shout get out get out where's the doors where which way get me out of here.

The morning after the concert I take a bus into Boston Centre walk out to Back Bay. I watch a man in eighteenth-century fancy dress shout to a tourist group danger danger English warships approaching look LOOK far out to sea can you all see? Fancy dress man laughs chucks cardboard Tea Box after Tea Box into Back Bay water plop splash. Fancy dress man roars more laughs shouts there goes your Tea goodbye Tea there it goes. Tourist crowd disappear look cheated. Fancy dress man disappears. I lie down on duckboards my head on a typescript. The Nuremberg war crime trials opening speech lent to me by the Nuremberg chief prosecutor to read. I go to sleep in hot sun beside Back Bay oily water.

A man touches my shoulder. He wakes me says lying there I am in danger of sunburn. He is fixing his motorboat tied to the jetty. He's been watching me. He will go back to his apartment fetch me a sunhat. He goes away and comes back. He carries a blue denim peaked cap. He says his three friends are coming to fix their boat. Turns out their boat can't be fixed. They'll go fishing in his boat. They invite me along.

The four men have a crate of beer. Talk about a recent Boston murder trial. A man invited two girls to go fishing. Out at sea he attempts to kill both girls. The four American young men rock our boat laughing. Say that might happen to me. Out at sea. With them today. Our power boat passes close below warehouse high brick walls. Windows broken. Iron gantries stick out. The men tell me in World War II ships carrying food medicines clothes left this warehouse to join convoys crossing the Atlantic Ocean from Boston to England. Hunted day and night by Nazi U-boats. I think of my gentle-natured socialist uncle who captained Atlantic convoy ships. He stayed alive.

A white motorboat shows further down the Bay. The young men yell it's Hank's the bastard keep away we gotta keep away. I say why? Hank's my sister's husband he gives her grief that bastard ain't never gonna fuck my sister about no more that's damn well damned for sure. I ask why? He says one night my sister and me are over at our Ma's I lift her house keys out've her purse I go over to Hank's place I hide good till that bastard comes home and some more until he's sleeping then I go in the bedroom I'd got a real sharp knife I put the blade down gentle at Hank's throat I say wake up now Hank do it nice slow and easy or else you ain't never gonna wake up again that bastard opens his eyes starts to open his mouth I say don't talk Hank cos I've got this pretty girl close up against your neck if you even shiver I don't think I can stop her from taking a bite outta your throat Hank stares right up at me I tell the bastard no more never again messing with my sister Hank you agree okay? The bastard blinks his eyes I just keep my knife on his windpipe for a while so he won't forget then I leave. The young men in our boat laugh more drink more beer agree Hank's an asshole and a jerk.

Our boat powers off to where effluence dashes out from a factory water system. No fish surface. The young men tell me we're not gonna fish no more we'll take you somewhere special we'll put you right on your plane back to England. They all laugh the boat roars across dark brown water to where the airport's international flights runway sticks out into the Bay. The boat anchors close to airline landing slab several highways wide. The young men gulp beer. Each time a jet plane comes in to land all four stand up scream wave arms at plane so low overhead silver underbelly so wide sky disappears. Airplane engine loud even louder than I think hell is. A huge wind blows I scream too I'm terrified near my face vast silver wings. Underneath my ears ache my voice howls my eyelids hurt teargassed pain.

The four young men leave me back safe at the boat jetty. I take a bus out to the airport. I board a plane and sleep my head sideways on cabin fleur-de-lis washable wallpaper. As dawn begins Ireland's Emerald Isle so green so far away is below. My plane home.

– Herself –

How could she think about herself when he was out there somewhere. Where was he now this minute. This moment. Was he alive. Happy. With his friends. Or was he alone. Without money and without her. Really he's a selfish man. Absorbed. Yes that's the way to look at it. His story and hers. He wouldn't let her be herself. Brute he was. Then she begins to cry. Not sobs. Tears on her cheeks on both sides of her face. She lets the wet sensation be. I'm not going to wipe my tears away. That's what he wants. He wants my sorrows wiped away with the back of my hand. Like a loving gesture. Spontaneous gestures of love. Well he's not having that. I'll do the washing up. Tears dry all on their own. I'm not feeling sorry for my tears.

The water is cold then warm then hot. She flicks her fingers in running water and thinks I wish I knew how to play the piano and sees herself through an open window from the street playing swaying forward and back as pianists sway in concerts bowing to the piano or to the music or to the composer or to their own fingers and hands.

Pianists are lucky she says aloud and she looks up at the kitchen window and thinks what is happening now why am I wishing if only someone will hear me washing up and look in and say I like the sound of your hands dipping in and out of water the slight difference when your fingers are in bubbles on the surface to when your fingers dive and water breaks open and your hands become visible.

No I have never wanted to be a pianist before she hears herself say and she splashes washing-up water bubbles on window glass so she can't see clearly what's going on in the street and for the millionth time she feels angry that she ever went to Ireland. Her first time journey was rainy hilarious and she smiles and jingles forks and knives about in the bottom of the washing-up bowl her fingertips in bubbles not so white now leave lakes between bubble islands that part drift twist bump into different islands or the same island in a different place.

On the Irish train from the east coast to the west she begins to read *The Mill on the Floss.* Or rather she remembers she read half a chapter and stopped. The story was too slow for me. Yes that's what the problem was. The-Mill-on-the-Floss. Even the title sounds slow as if mill water won't move. If she'd kept on with the story. If she had not stared at the green wet fields and grey wet stones and wet animals and hens. If she hadn't thought I'll think of him instead and shut her eyes and there he is opening a door and leaning a little bit forward and looking as nice as pie the cat that got the cream and she's the cream. Then not bored any more she'd gone to sleep and woke as her head jerked bump-bump at stations and she had only one thought. Not yet. Not yet. And she slept on. The bump-bump-not-yet-not-yet's carried on and then she wakes up and it is still raining and starting to get dark and it is her station and there he is leaning a little forward and he takes her suitcase and in the car along the black roads sheep's eyes lit up electric bright and he says he'll read *The Mill on the Floss* with her and she can have a hot bath before supper and there is the house and the door and the woven straw hall carpet and up the stairs and in her room he puts down her suitcase and she doesn't know if this is when a kiss should begin so she turns away to the suitcase and her thumbs press shift silvery little knobs so silvery tongues flick up. She lifts the suitcase lid and he and she see folded Priest's clothes.

He and she laugh so much they dance in the bedroom dancing up against each other and dancing apart and lifting out a Soutane and a white dress thing and another and a green and gold embroidered long sash and black shoes and socks and another black dress and grey wool nearly worn out knickers and a black wood cross with a silver Jesus crucified on one side and a leather prayer book and a Bible and a photograph of a large white building with statues erect along the roof.

Look he says it's the Vatican in Rome.

What shall I wear tonight she says? The black? Or the white? Which do you like me in best?

They hold up Priest's clothes by the shoulders and whirl as if the Priest is with the two of them dancing. She winds a green and gold sash round and round her waist and then he takes the end and pulls and she twirls and spins and the sash unfurls and falls on the carpet and they sit on the bed and she folds the green and gold and he says what can we do and she says I wonder where my clothes have gone and he says yes I'll go and telephone the station it's not late yet someone might still be there.

She stays at his house for a week and everyone who

comes to see him is told about the Priest's clothes till her dresses seem slightly disappointing and even slightly odd after the story has been told again and again and whoever is listening says I wonder whether the Priest tried your dresses on and they laugh at that picture.

Her hands are in flat water now the bubbles are gone it's flat transparent water and he's gone that is what many men do. First it is her father who goes and then her man and now her son's gone. Why do men have to go or why do they stay. That's easier. They stay for food and clean clothes and all the listening and them not speaking or sulking and getting their own way. Who knows what happens in the head of a man who doesn't get his own way. Something frightening or a message like a verb he has learned at school. I am. You are. He is. I am not enjoying this. You are not enjoying me. He is gone and now across the road. I don't care about across the road. She dries her hands and takes the kitchen scissors and pulls at a fistful of hair and cuts and another fistful and another and she goes into the bathroom and looks in the mirror and cuts and says goodbye hair.

At the greengrocers a woman queuing in front of her gestures then says go on ahead of me you're in a hurry go on now sir. Then the woman sees a woman not a man beside her. And the two women laugh and say it doesn't make any difference. Really it doesn't.

– Lester –

Saturday 31st October 1992. I think this is what happened. Racing in Miami Florida USA a racehorse's thin legs suffer injuries on hard racetracks made of rubber wax and sand spread onto asphalt. Pale and hot Lester Piggott eleven times our UK champion jockey will ride Rodrigo de Triano in the big race. Lester the old man is fifty-seven now. Been drumming rocking swaying slapping racehorses under him forty-five years most days of most every year tuned to each horse's faster and faster breaths. Three intakes of air a second at a flat-out pace. Lester is five foot eight inches. Tall as I am. We stand taller than jockeys and most women and that's why if a woman is at home and she watches daytime television it's Lester's bum that's higher than the others she can identify and she bets housekeeping cash on him to win to buy her things she wants. Cantering down to the start gate his knees and thighs grip as he kneels on his feather-light saddle crouched in perfect rhythm with a thoroughbred's long strides. Maybe like he does with girls.

Miami racetrack air fills with dust. In the race before the big race Lester rides Mr Brooks a gelding strongly medicated by Bute painkiller to ease injured muscle pain in the young horse's legs. At twenty-five miles an hour speeding on a left-hand bend Lester born partly deaf but all the same suddenly hears a bone snap sound. Imagine half a ton of horse ninety degrees heat real hard track rushing by. His arms and elbows pull on reins to put pressure on his horse's velvet lips. Hold-up-hold-up he mutters. He sits low on the saddle now his thighs clench his glance back was to see how many horses' hooves might trample him when his three-legged horse takes the fall it must. Ten horses is forty hooves. Four-three-two only one second now to prepare. On my television I see his shape shift over to one side on his saddle. His judgement about which side he hopes to fall clear. I see him start to slide arms wide down his horse's flat shoulder disc. Caress his horse's neck like a jockey riding into the winner's enclosure. Then horse scaffold topples no seconds left no more decisions as pay dirt hits. I say to my television what if Lester dies he always was a quiet one hardly ever smiled he'd be quiet forever. Lester Piggott the man with a face like a well kept grave I've heard said.

In the ambulance Lester opens his eyes. His racehorse trainer daughter Tracy is with him. He asks her what won? Tracy says I don't know but you'll be okay dad. Lester whispers holy cow don't you know the bloody winner. You're my daughter.

But I don't know if Lester is alive. I'm four thousand miles away in England. I turn off the television. I feel a fear of dying. Nothing special about me. My love for Lester. I hardly ever go racing now. I watch him a few times each flat-race season. Now and then I dream I'm him again fast as the wind as me and a pony race alone over ancient Cotswold grasslands skylark songs high above in blue skies and I call to the lovely hills *Look at me . . . I'm Lester . . . I am Lester Piggott.*

– What the Children Like to Do –

The ninth floor of a monster glass concrete hotel downtown. Awake at 2 a.m. Next door are three twelve-year-old girls in their heaven. Any one night deal in any affordable hotel will do. One street away from our house uptown is a hotel the girls most wish to stay in. If it was cheaper I say. I keep our downtown destination a secret. When I lose my way on the Isle of Dogs driving through a sewage smell the girls all say this is a GREAT PLACE to stay NOT is it REALLY EXPENSIVE can we park here and walk NOT.

When we at last get to the hotel downtown they walk into a gold foyer. Fake gold chandeliers plastic antlers on walls fake Chinese urns tall as my girls fake shiny square marble pillars Hotel Fake. The girls stare gasp say oh-hh wow-ww AMAZING. I've got to go back home I've got to get cool stuff to wear. I'm staying here. Do you think. It's ama-a-zing. When the swimming pool has chunks of tiles missing and the jacuzzi isn't working and they're not allowed in the steam and sauna the girls say the water in the pool's REALLY warm really really REALLY warm.

When there's no extra bed in their room they say it doesn't matter. We'll all sleep in the big bed. We're not going to go to sleep at all anyway. No we're not. What's the point of sleep.

When dinner takes forty minutes to arrive they take

photos of each other to show off their hotel coiffured hair-dos. They pose and say we're The Quiff Sisters. No we're not we're the Quiff Sissies. You're our Quiff Mother. Hi Quiff Mum. No she's not she's our aunt. Hi Aunty Quiff.

In the dining room are black and purple wallpaper walls and ceiling and tablecloths and napkins to match purple and black carpet colour. Xeroxed Matisse and Cézanne pictures and other great modern artists hang in fake gold frames. An adult couple stare at the girls and leave before us. The girls say did you HEAR him say it's RIDICULOUS to bring THEM here. She STARED at us as if we're FILTH. Did you see her SKIRT slit up to HERE she points at her own waist. The girls are laughing. There are twenty-three empty tables in the room.

In the morning the girls say can we stay here for longer. Forever. Say yes. Please please. Can we. You can go back home. And we'll stay here. Forever. For our whole lives.

– The Farm –

These days I often think of my spirit father my once a tortoise and before that the wind bossy know-all not there all the time father Hermit Jones.

I have to be careful how I describe him because if I get him wrong and he disappears then I am lonely because he will listen to my stories even when I can't find any words at all and breathe sadly and make shapes in the air by waving the palms of my hands while he laughs in a slightly false he's had one-too-many way and swears me always to tell the whole truth not the truth truth or the truthity-truth-truth and sings dance, dance, dance little lady so obsessed with second best you don't know who you are he tells me briskly to get a move on for heaven's sake he's heard Romany ponies have broken through and are grazing loose on our spring clover and where is Jake and will I damn well hurry up he calls me angel-eyes curly-top slow-coach coffee-houser says he will damn well find Jake himself I am to fetch halter ropes not go wandering off into the dark or he will send the damned sun and moon and the whole speechless shebang after me then I'll see all hell's to pay.

So Jake and I search hills around Ebony for Romany ponies. We scent honeysuckle clambering over sharp stone walls. In the dark we stop still as statues as pheasants scare shout out in night black trees. We sniff at the garlicky nearness of foxes and we look across stubble as a ghost white owl flies along the wood's edge. A spider trembles in its web near my face. We stand back to back against a tree and clasp fingers. A boy and girl tied together. We tramp across rabbit burrows. See rabbit eyes fat wet stares and rabbit petal ears. Tonight I hear particoloured Romany ponies stumble in soaking clover dew. In the dark the ponies graze my father's clover. Ponies' front fetlock hobble ropes linked by chains so a pony can't stray far away. Ponies nostril breath ruffles night air pony tails swish drum brush strokes ponies munch bass chords munch munch again again.

At supper in the house we eat four trout Jake caught in Fishpond yesterday. My mother is silent. My father curses his two missing toes cut off by teeth knives of his harvesting machine. Steel harvester knives cut wheat straw ears shake sieve separate corn from chaff. After rain showers oil spill drools from the sump makes the drum stick. My father is an impatient man. He kicks the drum to start up knives to slice off straw stalks. Since his accident he walks to one side. A furious lopsided limp.

I reach for greengages in a crystal glass bowl. Jake says to me tonight when it's dark I'll go up to Top Field. That way if there's any Romany dancing commotion going on the breeze will carry their music to me. You go and wait by the slip-rail gap. If you hear my nightjar call twice you cut the ponies' hobbles. Rope three as leaders. Head home. Ride one lead two. If you hear my owl hoot twice and twice again you go back to the gap. If I bark the fox there's trouble so you don't make a sound.

Jake and I have done this before. We have done other

things at night. We have circled Five Acre on foot. Whispered to Frenchman and Mercy. Held out white sugar lumps on palms of our hands. Heard ponies' hooves on earth near us. Felt ponies breath on our arms. Slipped webbed halters over silken pony ears. Vaulted astride and galloped the grey Mercy and the chestnut Frenchman across farmland in moonlight. Our ponies shy at shadows. Leap up over drystone walls. Our knees touch. The grey and the chestnut land together. The grey Mercy ahead in the valley. Frenchman quicker on the turns and stronger uphill. Our midnight steeplechase. One mile to Castlebarn. One mile back. Always the same prize. No one to know.

Afterwards the ponies sweat in ripples. We pull handfuls of dock leaves and cooch grass and rub lines of foam off sweaty necks. After the last time Jake says I want to bring a girl one night if you'll lend Mercy. I say I don't know. I don't know. Our arms draw circles along Frenchman's back. My arms cross his. Jake says that's enough. His fingers let drop warm green scrunched weeds. He holds my shoulders says show me I want to know.

– Trains and Buses –

Coming into Aberystwyth by train at a quarter to eleven at night I ask two Welsh girls pale as chalk in black tangled clothes where to find a place to sleep.

At this lateness . . . she'd best go down by the sea.

The sea. Downhill to the sea. Coloured lights bump the wind on a high wire. A man opens a hotel door looks me up and down says I don't know if we've a room disappears. I think what part of my life can I offer him as a proof of my honest character. What alliance with what style person place would reassure him. Better stay silent.

Aberystwyth to Cardigan green double-decker top front seat. Beautiful the sea blue and gold miles below cliffs twisting pale scarves along edges of green fields. Sheep and lambs pretty as knitted things for babies. Blackberry bushes ripening shiny cut back off roadsides for bus stops. Downhill s-bend swoops into villages. My white-knuckle ride.

Sat across from me is the only other bus passenger a blonde boy who eats munch munch his sweets and crisps never looks at the breathtaking view. Do you make this journey often I ask him longing for someone to sigh with. Yep my dad lives on a bit munch munch. It's wonderful I say they could charge a hundred pounds for it I reckon. S'pose munch munch. Does anything that grows familiar become unwatched. Marilyn Monroe. Adonis. Just figures around furniture. Just furniture. Nothing special. What keeps things special.

Now angry man gets on bus. Where's this bloody thing going to. I want to go to Cardigan. It doesn't say where it's bloody going. I say yes to Cardigan. It's okay. It's going there. Stay with me. You'll be ok. He mutters. He wants someone to yell at. Something in him is that angry.

By Aberystwyth station was Bygone Days a little house museum. A woman's life on show. Rooms full of radios knives forks spoons shoes tins kites bras knickers Merry Widow corsets dresses calendars carpets chairs ornaments bus tickets shawls petrol cans carthorse harness weed killers trowels basins recipes egg whisks buckets spades vests gloves saddles bridles racquets balls shorts tennis dresses swimsuits football shorts sunglasses spectacles straw hats caps top hats cloaks paints toys teddy bears dolls xylophones a piano a switchboard black and white photos in albums newspapers magazines cookery books encyclopaedias. Her life piled up hung nailed spread out. Amazing. How could she use see touch smell taste throw catch sit on lie on walk in stand under so many things.

The Fishguard to St. David's bus driver is eating an ice-cream. It is a fruity pink. I say that looks good. He says why don't you get one over there in that shop. An Everything Shop. Cakes one side. Papers and paints things for entertaining children. Writing letters learning a foreign language the other side. Ice-cream in a cold box at back. A white-haired lady slowly moves cardboard boxes off the cold box. I do the same. I put them in the wrong place. She puts them back on the cold box. She moves them again herself. I get anxious not to be too long. I say I'm on the St. David's bus. The driver has my things. He said to come here for an ice-cream. She says tell him if he goes without you he'll never get an ice-cream here again.

The bus ticket machine has broken. Our driver blames another driver. Says bloody man's got a hand like a bloody hammer breaks the bloody thing every time he uses it bloody idiot. The only other passenger points to a river we're crossing.

Says I was baptised in there. I say underwater. She says yes we all are. Everyone round here is. She points at a row of cottages says Saturday one of those girls is getting married Saturday after that the girl two doors down every Saturday it happens. I say that will be nice for them. They'll all have babies and they'll have friends to talk to. She says they've got babies already.

I call a taxi number from St. David's Information Centre. A London black taxi comes. Driven by a girl. I stare. She says it's from Manchester we've only had it a month. She drives very slowly. We pass St David's huge cathedral the ruined Bishop's Palace necklace of arches high up linking different bits of monks' lives by a balcony pathway. We go out into the country towards the sea.

On my Fishguard to London train home a *Daily Telegraph* racing photographer says Lester Piggott he's a legend . . . isn't it. I ask him about how Bute works. He says it's medication they use in America to dull pain in horses' legs. American race course tracks are made so hard you don't expect a two-year-old to last a year racing on those surfaces. In California when they want to break a racing record they scrape a top layer off the track so horses go extra speed any legs are wrecked in the one race. Curves against the sky appear out of the train window after hours of flatness. Why do hills mean so much to me. Why do my spirits lift. As if a journey will begin. Paths. Difficulties are visible. In my imagination a summit might be achieved. Hills. I must have hills. Or things in me will die.

On a station platform two women meet up. A mother and her daughter. The mother white-haired the daughter middle-aged. White-haired woman is excited. Her smiles. Her shiny eyes. Her nods. Yes yes. I have this girl. My girl. My daughter. The love of my life. Come to visit. Yes and years of lonely. Fifty years and all the hours of missing her. Of things breaking. Cups necklaces fingernails necklaces bike chains her heart. Someone to hold again. My daughter is come back. Her face is here her eyes her hair they are mine again. I am again. They are laughing. Today she's a mother. One more time. Someone says John was a silent man that's why I married him and that's why I left him.

Underground train. Tired people. Faces tipped down. A neck slopes forward skin hangs in little festoons. This tube is nearly airless. Used air. Not nice to breathe. Platform lit but dark. Coming off at King's Cross I hear music lots of music. From another land where music is for dancing flirting touching calling. In front of buskers I fumble for money. He plays the accordion. She plays a guitar. She bows now and then. He dips down on his knees.

I get to the top of the escalator and look back. Near me a woman stands a brown-checked jacket pinched tight under breasts and flared over her hips. She watches the musicians.

I watch her. Her thoughts are faraway. At home. In another country. In mysteries of landscape and other things. She turns quickly. I say it's lovely music. She says yes. It's beautiful. I say where are you from. She says Greece our music it is lovely. I say I was watching you wondering if it reminded you of home. She says ours is more Balkan there's Samba in it. We are so suddenly happy. Two women in the underground. Thinking of dancing. And love. She says I play the accordion you know and when we go into the hills for a festival it is always with the accordion for music you know. I say yes. I have never been up into hills for a festival although somewhere in me I have. Many many times. Festivals. This is a festival. For a few moments. She says I must go to work. I say me too. She says goodbye. I say goodbye.

– Heron –

I am going to forget Muskrat my hero for now and just listen to the wind in the heavy soaking trees and the occasional blackbird. There is a heron I can see flying near a river. I don't know who noticed it first. The man stood beside me or me. He has good eyesight. I am shortsighted and wear dark glasses with rose brown lenses and depth vision. Looking through my lenses I see the skies much as J.M. Turner painted skies. Clouds radiant as flowers. I read J.M. Turner never missed a sunrise or a sunset in all his long working life unless he was ill or travelling so I began to do the same. If you want to learn go to the masters obviously. When I get over the disappointment of Muskrat if I do because it is not so nice to create someone and then not know what happens to them. I mean if there is a death it is I who have killed. I try to make a sunrise happen.

Through the lenses of my glasses I live a little in the future. Summer is more russet. Autumn light is thick and dark. Winter is rosy. Spring is dry and burnt in places. I think I see the heron first but that opinion could be because of this habit I've gotten from wearing the glasses. We both certainly looked up at the sky and adjusted our ideas pretty quickly of what a heron pursued in flight does. The man and I say to each other isn't it extraordinary amazing why do crows chase a heron?

I must learn to listen more carefully. I know the man

said it's like watching a dogfight up in the sky at the Battle of Britain because I remember then I made the heron into an airplane. And then into a dog. And then the rhythm of Bird Dog came to me out of the blue. Johnny is he's a bird Johnny is a he's a dawg hey bird dawg. I keep quiet about Johnny Bird Dog because if the heron gets injured by the crows while the man and I are laughing at a song then maybe the man and I have something nasty in common with the crows that are attacking the heron.

He and I stare up at the sky. We watch the crows dash in close pecking to injure the heron. The heron is tired and vexed. The big grey bird fast flies down long blue sky slopes. The heron's flight flattens out parallel to brown ground to be safer flying low. The crows are black water runnels rushing down a dry stream jinking this way and that around invisible rocks. I make the heron into an empty dress with high shoulders and wide flapping sleeves crossing the sky. Then I turn the big bird into a spirit. A soul in a struggle to be alive between earth and heaven or hell. Then into a fast skier using gravity's whoosh as impetus to climb the sky again. The pair of black crows attack in harmony in jerky rhythms. Violent music rhythms. Punk jab jabs at a pale grey dress.

When I exaggerate the actual size of the heron that thought turns the bird into a cylindrical corpse tapered to points at each end laid out on a flat blue sky. Two miniature black hyenas snatching at a corpse.

Henri Matisse says I paint the emotion the table produces in me. It must be fear pushes the tired heron to fly higher maybe than the big bird has ever flown. The grey frayed wings flap slower till halfway up a vertical rise the wings appear to break. Is it complex or only exhausting for a heron to hold a vertical flight-line. I wish this man was more informed. The heron travels upwards brilliantly straight with enormous effort. It hurts me to watch. I want to reach into the sky and put my arms around the heron fold up its legs that dangle below appearing as internal organs starting to fall out. Thin heron neck waves snakeish in the sky. A snake curled up asleep on a big bird's back now wants to get down on ground level. Heron-beak lunges at a crow. Another celestial ascent begins.

The man says why are the crows being so aggressive? The heron is not carrying a fish. What will make the crows leave the heron alone? He is fond of crows but he likes them a great deal less today. I who am only fond of crows because he is fond of crows relapse into thinking they are gratuitously aggressive shiny black birds that remind me of being scared in streets on dark nights. Crows watch people like I sometimes watch a person to enjoy fear.

Heron and crows swoop from vertical flying away along a shallow horizon towards a far-off field of green wheat. The man and I walk a hard mud track through scents of foxtail grasses and cow parsley. My girl days dream had a church all creamy lace cow parsley blossom for my wedding. We stand on a bridge over a stream. We talk about clues why what is happening began. The heron and the crows are hidden. I stare into an oak tree. I see a fish lie twitching on a branch. That is what I want to see. I have become less fond of the man. He knows so little about the behaviour of crows and herons even although he always creates a crow on tall elegant china clay pots he throws.

– Outside –

If I suddenly wake up in the night I panic is it a burglar? Is the dog barking downstairs? In the street cars arrive. Full on rock music rattles my toothbrushes. This means summer weather drunk stoned youth is out to have fun in the park. The music stops. Car doors crash shut. Fuck you no fuck you wanker what's that nothing loser get off me no fucking good it fuck is I'm telling you give me that they shout. A long scream ends in laughter or vomit.

I rub my eyes and put on a white towelling dressing gown over long white nightdress in the dark and go downstairs where the dog is. Come on Sam. Sam keeps his nose down on his paws. Come on I say I can't go out alone.

Boys stagger about by the park gates shout at Sam and me hey see that a fucking ghost with a fucking dog fucking ghosts don't have fucking dogs it's fucking coming fucking hell. Two boys reel off the park bench towards me and the dog yell Sam Sam Sam come here Sam you okay Sam? I see one's a girl her panda eyes her black platform laced boots she sways close yells in my face sorry sorry really sorry is Sam okay? shush I say there's a new baby upstairs go further away go to the fourth bench up the park then we won't hear you Sam's fine go on go now. The girl waves her arms herds the boys up the park shouting fucking move can't you hear me you fucking deaf? One boy grey hoodie pulled down over his face stays hunched sat on the back rail of the first bench snarls at the girl fuck you I'm warning you you got to talk nice to me leans my way you don't fucking talk to me okay do you hear I want you to use proper language fuck off. I say you're a funny boy. I turn out of the park call Sam Sam this way Sam trots up to the furious boy on the bench the boy looks down at Sam says fucking pisser I whistle for Sam. Voices up the park call bye Sam night Sam.

Upstairs I don't turn on the bedroom light. I hear breaking glass and voices further off a lot quieter. Sam's downstairs he'll bark if they come near the house. I go back to sleep.

When I open my eyes it's daylight. That's a surprise. Boys on drugs usually wake up the street again when they leave the park. Maybe Sam calms them. Takes them out of themselves a bit. Maybe a dog should wait for them at the park gate every night the weather's fine. Spilt garbage around the bin is a problem Sam could get sick eating that. I can ask for a bigger garbage bin. I've already asked twice this summer. I asked last summer too.

– After the Pop Concert –

At night in the snow at the Albert Hall the pop concert ends and girls hundreds of teenage girls exit under streetlights and start home. My two girls lean in the car window.

Can we stay around here for a bit
And get their autographs

I say have you got a pen.

We'll only be by that door over there
Please say yes
Oh great it's cool
Come on
Quick quick

I say you need paper for your autographs.

No we don't we'll use our hands
And never wash it off
Never never

They run around the concert hall in the snow for one hour with other girls in little flocks like chickens towards worms.

There he is quick
Run run
Over there

Is it him John oh John over here
Terry it's Terry
It is yes it is
No it's not it's Brian
Bri-an Bri-an
It's not him
Yes it is
No it isn't
I swear it was
It wasn't it was a person
I'm going back to the other door
Which one
The door over there
Look someone's coming who is it
Quick it's Tony

Sam our golden dog and I saunter past girls in the snow or we sit in the car with the heater blowing full on. We watch our two girls climb up onto a flat-back truck parked at the back of the Albert Hall and I take photos of them as they reach up to pout kiss at Tony John Terry Brian. The boys are ten-feet tall plastic cut-outs stood loafing on the billboard. My girls wear pop-concert uniform short shiny silky flared skirts black tights thick soled white or black shoes black zip bomber jackets necklaces of key ring photos of the boys and old concert tickets. Love tat. The flat-back trailer floor is icy the girls shoes slip I call be careful move closer to the boys closer hold on tight to the boys. Gigantic security men in fat black puffer jackets patrol the Albert Hall circular walls. The girls plead with the men for information.

Which door will they come out of
You are Security aren't you
So you must know
You have to
It's your job it must be
So tell us please
Please oh go on
We won't tell anyone will we
Never

I see one of my girls kneel in the snow and apparently stroke a security man's leg.

What are you doing to his trousers
What is she doing to your trousers
He told me I can have his pass it's stuck onto his trousers it's been used but I still want it

The girls find a minibus parked close by one door.

Are you their driver
Are you
You are aren't you
Is this where they'll come out
Is it really
You've got to tell us
We won't tell anyone else
Never

The driver says if I tell you I'll lose my job won't I.

Will you will you really what will you do then
Where will you go how did you get this job

Do you like it I wish I had it
Oh yeah that would be cool

The concert ended at 11 p.m. At midnight there are fourteen girls and the dog and me left here. One girl is in a wheelchair. The others run past her from door to door. She swivels the wheels watches them run out of her sight around the curved wall. The minibus driver speaks to his mobile phone. At eighteen past twelve five girls are at the right door. Two of the boys come out. Security men say back now everyone stand back keep right back. In five seconds the boys are inside the minibus. In fifteen seconds they've gone.

I talked to John
You didn't did you what did he say
Nothing he saw me
Terry saw me
It was brilliant where were the other two
They left earlier
How d'you know
I don't
I'm starving
Can we get a pizza please please
Yes can we on the way home
It was really cool
Really really really

– Cigarettes –

Cigarette smoking is a lost joy now. I love the short violent intake of drugged air the languorous gestures. But the risk is too threatening. Slowly the poison the whole blood stream fills. The waste remains, the waist remains and kills. My small son implores me each night at bedtime please don't kiss me you smell of tobacco and anyway I don't want to get too fond of you because you'll die of cancer soon. I kiss him anyway.

There was a girl who was hypnotised to stop smoking. She was very sceptical but it worked for her friend. She threw away all the cigarettes in the house and took a train to town for her first hypnosis session. After some time on the hypnotist's couch listening to promises she did not believe the hypnotist repeating You will never want to smoke. Never again. No wish no desire. Never ever again. She sits up makes her apologies and says she will pay now for this one session and not come back again. That hypnotism is not for her. She says she is sorry.

The hypnotist says she owes him fifty pounds cash payable now. Or a hundred pounds card or cheque. She doesn't have fifty in cash. Her voice rises to extreme anger. She argues and shouts at the hypnotist for longer than the time left of her appointment. She is furious at the unfairness. She leaves the hypnotist angry. Longing for a cigarette. No time to buy a packet. The argument makes her late for her next event. A committee meeting. The committee are waiting for her not pleased the meeting will begin late and end late. She hurries to the train station. She's missed the train to her local station. She catches a train to a station further away from her home. No time to buy cigarettes. Rain is pouring down when she gets off the train. She joins a queue for a taxi home. She asks the man stood behind her to keep her place in the queue while she buys cigarettes. He says no. He will not. So home again no cigarettes. She sleeps and dreams about how she fights the hypnotist. Next morning she considers the awful day before and she reckons if she can survive such a day with no cigarette then she can survive any day. So she stops smoking.

At a party some non-smoking years later she is offered a cigarette. She says yes thank you and the next day she buys her own cigarettes and starts smoking again. That week by chance she meets the original friend who told her about the skill of the hypnotist. Her friend says did you see what happened to our hypnotist? So sad. He died. His obituary was in *The Times* yesterday. He died on Monday. She remembers last Monday. The day she'd started smoking again.

I tell this story to a photographer. We sit opposite each other in a rowing boat on a beautiful lake. The photographer listens. I think how his intent gaze must be the way he adjusts what he sees in his camera lens. The photographer says to me, so did her smoking again really kill the hypnotist?

– A Fall –

I am here I am here I do not dare to call to a girl I don't know driving her car touching her gold shell earring with her finger and thumb passing a bus I am on I look down at her through two glass sheets and yes we smile close as forever angels in gnomonic time lovers alive alive-oh you are beautiful and me heading out the way girls do all smooth inside nylon on the run from staying home with him who breathes phlegm nonsense in his dreams gaarglyshlock ratter ratter he mutters over and over in the dark as we curvsy girls come indoors off rain yellow streets up the stairs singing Needles and pins yeah that's how it begins.

Earlier today all of a sudden I see my friend I say to her oh there you are where've you been it's days I've been calling you and no reply she says sorry I'm really sorry and in her eyes I see tears she says he I it's not only you I mean I must hurry back I must go so I ask where's your car can you carry this for me it weighs a ton have you got your red Fiesta that one a car salesman told you had all the toys? she says he uses it now I say why where's his own car? she says Franco has it he's out of work again I say Franco that man is Mr Lazy London the World the Universe.

She laughs suddenly sweetly our fingers lock past times come back sleepover nights pony patterned duvets and pinned to bedroom walls James Dean's I'll never love again grainy paper eyes and Let me take you there and Sergeant Pepper and Let me hold your hand turned up high and now our hens' feet upside down hands lug plastic shopping bags.

Why've I've got such muchos stuff but she's got none I'm thinking why it's I got the cash stuff 's everywhere in every window in our hometown pay less have more you are we know you are not poor come in yes so I go in shops I paw all what's there it all can be mine then sleep will come so I'll not hear him when he snores.

Two grown up girls we are today not saying words then I say you didn't tell about him she says you didn't ask so hell's bells to you I say it's okay the blind white fish are frying nicely and I chant liar liar pants on fire she yells smokey knickers now you're talking I say come on let's take an hour together we'll flag a taxi down we'll go to Old Hernando's Hideaway then on the pavement us two sing aloud *I know a dark secluded place A place where no one knows your face A glass of wine a fast embrace It's called Hernando's Hideaway olé All you'll see are silhouettes And all you'll hear are castanets And no one cares how late it gets Not at Hernando's Hideaway olé* I say look that taxi's stopped he's seen us wait look the old fellow's getting out he's fallen down he's in the soup Jesus Christ let's dump this stuff. We run to him we turn him over oh god his face is filthy I can't find his pulse where is it where where keep trying I'll call 999 can you hear his ticker?

Kneeling in road slush my friend puts her one hand on top of her other hand her fingers splay on the ribcage of old fallen man she presses down lets go presses down lets go chants one-two one-two and on grit pricks her bare kneecaps why've his lips gone blue she looks up says I can't do mouth to mouth must she kiss this fallen sag-cheeked stubbled soldier my friend starts a moan-singsong I join in Walk ON through the RAIN walk ON through the STORM and you'll NEVer WALK aLONE.

Police car is here. I call out police police. One kneels on tarmac by our old man. My friend keeps at his heart a policeman gets out a pocket mirror puts glass to our fallen soldier's mouth says no mist that means he's dead. You can stop now love. She says I don't want to I can hear him breathing the policeman says it's old air you're pumping out of him.

I reach down take my friend's hands say stand up love the old fellow didn't stand a chance. Another policeman says most likely gone by the time you began. Then we all see a teeth gum smile jink-jink across tarmac between shoes. That's dentures someone says. A young man picks up wet pink white thing comes up close to dead old man looks down sees says it's my dad. We a small crowd stare we watch time stop start again who will this young man be for the rest of today for forever changed now his brain tells a new sad chapter.

We two girlfriends go off away in the springy spongey bouncy cab the old man fell from my friend weeps I give her my blue handkerchief I cut from my favourite silk shirt when it wore out I say here sweetheart dry those tears we'll all die someday she says save for Jesus who lives forever so your mother used to tell us I tell her here lean on me stay quiet for a minute you always did talk too much an' me as well.

Quietly close we sit bump bumping along streets until I see Old Hernando's I say here we are let's get cheese on toast and tea she says I don't know I'm out of money and

I shouldn't wonder you are too with all you've bought and as well it's trouble at home if I get later than I said I'd be I say why why do you stay with him she says I get so many thoughts I do different things I say kill him I'd've she says no you'd not I can't go away leave him then send the children to be alone with him so I count time I see the swallows come and go then it's Christmas again I've got some stuff to help if the days get long I say let me see your arms no tracks at least she says remember the pigeons flying round and round above us while we lay in buttercups the stuff I take is like pigeons flying I nearly shout at her don't take that stuff she says I don't take it all the time I ask doesn't he notice what's going on she says he gets home gets his whisky turns on TV he's all done except for bets on horses dogs cars he'd bet on beetle races on any old thing not anything not what I read soldiers did to pregnant women got put in a barn then the soldiers threw dice I say what for she says on a girl or a boy baby born they'd pull a baby out to see who'd won.

I'm frightened I ask my friend is this the pills talking right now no one we've ever heard of does those things what's happening in your head? She is silent then she whisper hums I will rock you rock you I will cut you mend you I'm no use any more and I ask her where are the children right now this minute.

I tight lip anxious smile she says the children are at my mum's they're great it's I myself am at a loss if I have the day out all I am is in the shops with no surplus of cash after the small amount he doles out I get so down I don't know where to go if I stay home it's he doesn't speak to me that's hard.

I beckon a waiter I say thanks can we have two glasses

of champagne please we're celebrating she says it'll only start me off again some days I'll cry if someone asks in a fierce voice pass the salt our champagne arrives I say look in this glass see it fizz I can clearly see both our futures sparkle in those bubbles you better believe me I know it'll come true my friend blinks tears away I spoon swizzle champagne and say I'll give you taxi money you be sure to answer me when I call tomorrow or I'll just keep on calling come on let's drink up this champagne quick so you'll get home on time.

– Hospital Notebook –

Don't take me back to hospital please. Not to number thirteen unlucky ward. Let's go please let's go on up to a higher level. I've nearly died in here once I can't do dying again.

Walk keep walking along corridor pass STOP STEALING FOOD FROM THIS KITCHEN stuck on staff kitchen door.

Years ago in a hospital lift a card by the wall spin dial telephone read IN CASE OF CARDIAC ARREST DIAL 5-7-3-2-1-8-9-6 surely someone'll die dialing a number that long.

Thirteen floors below gold city lights sparkle. Eight million people down there alive. Hope I'll be. Ambulances drive in and out of darkness one two three.

A patient says these doctors say I'm depressed you'd think by now they'd have worked that out.

I ask her how long have you spent in hospital she says all in all counting other rare disease hospitals twenty-seven years.

Early morning plane turns across blue skies. I can see home from here. Suddenly I miss my childhood farm.

Mr Big Nurse says I never let women have the last word dear I'm one of those dear you'll never get the last word dear waggles fingers I say you haven't seen me before he says how do you know I say because I haven't seen you and off he whirls.

One patient has her arm hung inside a blue box on a hoist above her face. She says I say to doctors it's no good being friendly if you can't mend my arm.

Rare Disease patient moans my ribs are cracking.

Mr Big Nurse says tea? I say yes please any way it comes I like it strong. He says you said any way it comes you ladies always changing your minds. He prances away sings people do say I am a one. Blue Box Arm tells Rare Disease get them to give you the highest pain control. Rare

Disease says I have they don't listen. Blue Box says write it down. Rare Disease says I do.

A man sits by his wife's bed all night. Rare Disease says husbands don't do so well on their own sometimes I've sat all night with husbands when wives go into theatre or can't be visited in intensive care.

I tell my daughter on the phone it already feels like I've been in here a million years.

Little Mary hunches over the tea trolley. I say d'you have any fruit today please Mary. Mr Big Nurse looks down at her says you're supposed to have fruit at breakfast. Mary's fist flies at his nose.

Rare Disease says my prof put his long needles in me I was his last patient he took me across the road to the pub I said what's the point of taking me to the pub I don't drink I only go to play darts.

I say to Mr Big Nurse I can see my house from here he swivels stares at London below says there's a nice tent is that yours.

A plastic surgeon in a tailored suit washes his hands. Glances at Rare Disease. She says watch him bend over my bed. I tell him I'm getting old I can't stand it. Once I asked him have you had plastic surgery yourself do you fix up each other's faces all you doctors.

A physio works on Blue Box Arm asks is that ok for you. Physio girl doesn't seem to notice intense pain. It happens in hospitals a kind of hardening I'm always a bit scared.

Rare Disease says to Blue Box did you tell them your arm feels hard like it's wood. Blue Box says I keep repeating my arm feels like wood my arm feels like wood her arm poised to smack her face.

Mr Big Nurse collects used bed sheets says 50p a bag to wash them then they don't come back clean that brown bit's old we've had sheets with wee marks. A door slams he spins round says Health and Safety will go mental if they hear that.

I shuffle along linoleum underneath dimmed night time ceiling lights shuffle stop shuffle stop. Nausea keeps me awake. Intense nausea happens after your pancreas is taken out. I shuffle past worn out machines cracked rubber orange tubes looped in and out of pock-marked chrome two discarded mattresses wrapped in plastic lean against a wall. I shall walk out of here. A writer wrote surely of all the wonders of the world the horizon is the greatest. Someone calls out stop you're hurting me.Dolly ninety-three snores gently. Dolly not strong enough for surgery her snow-white hair pretty as a girl's.

Where is that doctor man. He said he'd give me my nausea medication by midnight. A nurse says he's gone for his break he's forgotten you. I hate that man I walk lean sit lie try to get my nausea to go away. I weep when is the doctor coming. The nurse says go back to bed I want you to understand here look on your chart you're not due medication. I weep I know I do know I understand but that doctor said he said I could have my medication early. Nurse says I have to ask a doctor on call tonight to write a prescription change your chart I want you to understand I say I do I do nurse sighs I'm sure as hell fed up with you big sigh takes key out of pocket unlocks cupboard hands me pills I sleep for half an hour.

Dolly hears my weeping says hasn't the doctor been yet I say no stupid man but they've got a lot of people to look after. I don't say to Dolly I hate him as much as I loathe nausea crave nausea medication the god of nausea this missing doctor is wherever he comes from whatever violence was maybe done to him his family village town wherever in the world doesn't concern me it's his pill I want not him he can pretty much die as he hands it to me for all I care I hate him.

I tell a junior doctor this blood pressure sleeve hurts his eyes blaze he argues back it does not I say please I am not criticising I am asking he says I have to concentrate on these things all the time so I do not make a mistake I say I know none of us knows how hard your work is really we don't I ask him if he has looked after a patient who's had my operation he says no he mostly looks after trauma I ask if he has a family he looks wary as if I might steal his children. I ask his children's names. He tells me. I ask their ages. He smiles a beautiful smile of a man thinking about love. I say there is nothing as wonderful as children is there.

A nurse tells me you must eat you must drink. I say Malek says I mustn't till my scan results come. She looks at my file says it says here. I say I don't know what to do. She sighs turns quickly her shoes squeak on speckled blue linoleum she leaves returns tells me I must not have food or drink.

A cleaner bangs a broom against my bed my bed legs shudder does she hate us and herself a dirty Styrofoam cup lies under a bed after she's gone. Perhaps she works here because she's desperate. I'd clean offices at night when no one's around a silent eerie job I did when I was seventeen.

Doctor teams walk corridors. Stop. Chatter chatter chatter. Honk honk honk. Patients wait.

How to escape intense sickening non-stop nausea. I strike out quick as a fish to my no nausea place. My fantasy nausea barrier a portcullis slice of steel shivers I am so sick of living in this nauseous place oh to sleep in No Nausea Land.

Malek sits by my bed brilliant intuitive focussed sparkly reeks tobacco Malek taps his forehead says you know what I think we have not the information we want the scan report the technician's report the real report not the doctors' report the doctors only look at pictures it is good but themtechnicians he sighs like a girl who's been happily kissed he says with no information we are firing an arrow but we cannot see where we must hit so the arrow will go anywhere. Malek I ask have you looked after patients who have had my operation before. His brown eyes look up at the ceiling he says like with half of my brain taps one side of his head repeats like half of my brain so now I am certain Malek will know what to do. Malek may I ask you he says please questions. I say my surgeon says a year from now I'll be able to do everything so what I want to learn I touch my fingers on Malek's brown arm is how to get from here to there can you tell me. Malek says you know what I tell my patients he stares in my eyes says go downstairs it is beautiful day here it is always the same look four beds the windows always shut go downstairs out out in air breathe air look around. Malek I will I say. He says another thing the first step is the hardest but then in a marathon the first kilometre is the hardest ouff-ouff everyone says the same push-push for a first kilometre always always the hardest so you go downstairs wait for the results take the painkillers. Malek I say my nausea medication I got frantic by midnight he says well the medication is three times a day if you take it more you will have a problem to whack. I laugh and he laughs too. Oh Malek I say it is so nice to laugh again thank you he gets up pats my arm I pat his arm he says you are sick of my ugly mug. I am not I say he says then that is why I shaved this morning we laugh happily oh Malek I say and he goes turns back says I am sorry you waited for your surgeon's team they have a very a very sick patient who has had the same operation as you. Later I ask Malek did the very ill patient are they better. Malek says no the patient did not live.

Dolly wakes up says you never know what's coming next do you it was my first time travelling it was when my husband was starting to get Alzheimer's you see so I went to Germany he was in the army there I thought here I am on the boat how will I know where to get off I follow a lady I saw on the bus she was wearing a fur coat I followed her around wherever she went and guess what happens she only takes her fur coat off doesn't she so I didn't know what to do did I. When I got there my husband was saggy as six he was overwhelmed unfortunately he's just that sort of person he takes everything to heart he said it was fate our granddaughter got killed the biker passed our house he wasn't on drugs or drunk he was just a mad driver he bashed into a tree that was very sad I never knew a funeral service like it people said their own thing fortunately my daughter's boyfriend's parents were so nice we never met them before and some of the boys my son taught sports to came and people from all over only last week one of them got in touch I thought well they must have thought a lot of her. I had a pleasant surprise today I thought today was Friday they won't come till tomorrow it turned out my son is off work today that was nice.

Not like when I came home from my cataract operation I looked in the mirror I said I can't believe how old I am my granddaughter just roared she said Gran you've always been that old I said to her not since I last looked I haven't.

Mother Ship Hospital sails along The Sea of Illness The Ocean of Distress.

Hospital translator Sam says he was born in India in the south I say the beautiful south he says so you know Thomas was born there yes born in our place Thomas the Disciple of Christ is buried in Madras. I say thank you for telling me.

Noreen from Labasheeda in Co Clare says Labasheeda means Bed of Silk says what's that you're writing takes my pen writes in my notebook Labasheeda Bed of Slick.

After Fumni and I make tea in the staff kitchen I sing see-you-later-alligator she pirouettes asks what's that. I sing in a-while-croc-o-dile-na-na-nah-nah. Fumni sways and in her black hair pink curls twirl.

A patient grumbles I want food I've been forgotten it happened before there's only fish left it's not right and I think about could any menu satisfy all eight hundred patients in the hospital.

My surgeon's team come to my bed. Sherrin rattles off on her fingers okay food okay digest okay clips taken out says I want to see the scar says scar okay says tests are clear. I say what did you say my tests are clear. Sherrin says yes back from the lab all clear I am crying oh oh that's wonderful that's so lovely the surgical team all laugh someone gets a tissue my fear of dying surfaces flies away. Sherrin says you're really doing really well. I see a junior surgeon remember him calm quick when I was very ill. I ask his name. He says Arenda 'Clinical Fellow'. He holds out his name badge. Says look I am 'Cynical Fellow'. We laugh at the printing mistake. I say to the team how long did my operation take. My so handsome Indian surgeon says six hours but we stopped for lunch. I say did you sit round me and eat sandwiches or did you go across the road to the pub. He stares. Irony is not for everyone

Nurse Jo says I'll leave this last stitch in. I say no don't please don't. Jo laughs says I did it just to see your reaction. Jo hugs me about my test results says you know I heard only yesterday I have a melanoma it isn't cancer but they want a test immediately I am very anxious I see so many people in here who. I say oh Jo I'm really sorry good luck.

As dawn breaks I listen to Dvorak the Martyr very wonderful choral singing. I remember my father's tenor voice singing opera arias in barns and stables on our farm remember my walk into hospital before my operation. I cried saying goodbye maybe forever to my beautiful daughter.

At night a red ribbon flutters twists above a building

site. I lean against the hospital main door. A young man walks toward me asks are you alright. I say yes I long for air there's a draught comes in the hinges of the door. He is a medical student. We talk about how some wards are in fact old peoples' homes how old people need a different kind of care how doctors sometimes don't like old people how doctors can be quite cruel. I shuffle back to the lift. Hear my own voice say please god make me well again.

I don't really want to talk to ill people now.

In the night a nurse brings a cup of tea I say that little blue-and-white pattern on the china is nice she says yes I don't know why they stamp NHS on it I say perhaps they think patients will steal cups and saucers she says yes run away with them down the street and I say or you'd go to tea with someone and we both say there'd be NHS cups and saucers we're so happy laughing.

Maybe it is now I am strong enough to pull a lid off a lunchtime fruit pot I am well enough to go home.

Today it's farewell and thank you hospital and thank you notebook. Writing has helped me to be alive in our dear world. Bless each person in this hospital who dies.

– Stay Alive –

I first see Chai Ling on television a bossy beautiful girl in Tiananmen Square she is leading fifty thousand student protestors she calls to her friends to stay together to stay strong to make peaceful demonstration to oppose their government's repressive laws her melodic voice grows tired her words rise in crescendos my television screen shows military tanks the students in heaps an arm a leg squashed. Two days later she disappears. News reports say that she's been killed by the Chinese Government authorities. Then her voice comes on the radio she says today is June 8 1989 it is 4 p.m. I am Chai Ling Commander-in-Chief of the Headquarters I am still alive.

The question is does she imagine even for one moment she is leading her friends to die or to be imprisoned as they bicycle towards Tiananmen Square so hopeful freedom will be in all their futures.

Innocence. The before. Not knowing.

I am in the trade of looking out for stories. I look for books that haven't yet been written. I say I am going to Hong Kong. My man says why. I say to try to find Chai Ling. He says who is Chai Ling.

I don't find Chai Ling in Hong Kong. I talk to Hong Kong journalists who shake heads say no news of Chai Ling. No news very bad. I ask college students are you fearful of what China will do to Hong Kong who nod heads say very afraid. One says you see hairs on my skin stand up when you ask. I search files a young English lawyer shows me about Vietnam Boat People who've escaped to Hong Kong no mention of Chai Ling among them. I ask a Singapore businessman in apparently the largest office in Hong Kong his windows look out over Hong Kong's wonderful harbour he says Chai Ling no I do not know anything about her.

A year later Chai Ling is in Paris. At 11.30 a.m. she will give a press conference close to the Arche de la Defense. In a Paris Métro tunnel suddenly we smell sewage. An orange felt-tip pen rolls across the floor. We all glance down. Then at each other. A man wearing earphones gestures to a man in a tracksuit to pick up the pen. A third man watches. No one has spoken. Earphones Man shrugs. Tracksuit Man checks our faces bends picks up the pen writes on the back of his hand leans his palm against the side too far away for me to read what he writes. Third Man is closer stares at the words for a moment. He leaves at the next station.

At the entrance to Chai Ling's press conference journalists queue up. I am not the friend who has lent me a press card nor am I the female journalist he borrowed the card from though I will say I am. The official at the door checking identities smiles. That's all he does.

In the top floor conference room the walls are dark silver blocks. Journalists spread up rows of seats in steep rising tiers folded newspapers bulge out of pockets camera lenses are taken out of steel boxes light meters and batteries are pulled out of flak jackets tripods' legs are extended tripods collapse there's a muddled feeling before Chai Ling appears.

White lights search for her. We stand up and screw our eyes tight to shield our sight of her from brightness. Journalists call out lay-dee lay-dee as if she is a pony. She sits down at a table. She wears a round neck red jersey. She smiles at us. A bride and her husband in Paris in springtime.

She reads written pages like a girl reading poetry aloud. Her cadence is lovely her words run liquid over harsh noises camera clicks knocks mutterings tripod legs are kicked out of the way a tripod steals another tripod's territory. Chai Ling's husband moves his chair closer to hers. He touches her arm quickly gently and she begins.

> In 1982 I was chosen by the League of Young Communists as one of the best model students in China. Now I am number four on the list of most wanted criminals. I haven't changed. I haven't stolen. I haven't killed. And obviously I haven't raped anybody. During the Tiananmen Uprising I rode my bicycle to join with other students in Tiananmen Square. As we pedalled along that morning we talked about what a student uprising in Tiananmen Square meant to us. About our ideals. About the careers we wanted. About how everything was going to change for the better. As we all pedalled to Tiananmen Square.

Her voice starts rushing angrily over stones of memory. She says at that time I did not understand why I was doing what I was doing. Now I understand it very well. We were testing the principle of peacefulness. The meaning of how to be a human being. The conscience it takes after forty years of dictatorship. How the old men of China don't understand they are confronting a generation brought up in the Cultural Revolution. With ideas about freedom and democracy. Now in China there is a conscience. And courage and vitality. There is a fight between life and death. And life wins.

Questions from journalists start. Do you have any news of Wang Deng. Did you see him while you were in hiding. Is he still alive. Chai Ling says I saw no other student I knew while I was in hiding. I have no news. All I can say to you is that as things are in China now one imagines the worst. The next question is it has been said that you are going to live in America. Is that where you feel you would be most effective. Chai Ling is tiring. She looks like a child a long way from home. Perhaps wishing she was home. Wishing like all refugees presumably do that she will not be away from home forever. She answers the America question says I don't know where that information came from we have not decided ourselves where it will be best for us but the French government has a long history of welcoming and assisting people like us from other countries.

An American journalist next to me whistles under his breath. I look at him. We both raise our eyes. But where is best for Chai Ling and her quiet husband to go. To live now. She makes an effort and her ballerina poise returns. Mercifully a row starts up about how one specific Students for Democracy movement is the best and truest. Chai Ling's husband shakes his pen at the speaker. We all turn towards a plump Chinese lady an older student leader. Chai Ling bows says you are the tidings of the 1950s. We all applaud. Chai Ling answers a last question. She says it is not true that Deng

Chou Peng's advisors came to confer with me. If only he had sent someone early enough.

The press conference ends. Chai Ling's husband holds up bold black typewritten words in English for the cameras.

OUR HEART IS A HEART OF STEEL
WHO IS THE MOST FEARFUL IS FEAR ITSELF
NO ONE PERSON CAN STOP THE MIGHTY CURRENT OF HISTORY

We pack up shuffle out. All of us older than these two we have listened to. Now a Chinese girl starts shouting at the front swings her body towards us back towards Chai Ling shouts why shouldn't I speak why shouldn't I why not why not. Cameras quickly circle her. Chai Ling's husband shows strength. He says the event is over that many people want the right to speak. He points at the many raised hands. He speaks in English. Chai Ling spoke in Chinese through one French and one English translator.

I leave tired and wishing things were different and that a camera had not fallen over just as Chai Ling asked her husband a question that Chai Ling had told us more of the story of her escape to Hong Kong her time in hiding her protection by Yellow Bird a secret organisation I've heard spirits students on the run away to other countries and I am disappointed at my own low spirits.

A ballet about Chai Ling is staged in Hong Kong to Handel's music. A prima ballerina is Chai Ling. She hides under a cloak at the finale. Chai Ling's own voice calls out I Am Alive.

– A Famous Man –

No one in my family is famous. In my kitchen on a shelf children can reach I keep small inherited silver things. Two silver compasses to save your life if you are lost. Silver finger tongs for stretching white kidskin gloves ladies used to wear at dances if glove fingers shrink after washing. A tiny silver wheel to roll along old paper maps to measure road distances. Silver snippers to cut off grapes. A concave silver cigarette case engraved with a motto FORK OVER FORK OVER and a lion rearing up behind a unicorn the motto bestowed by King Arthur of the Round Table after he ran away from an enemy and our ancestor forked hay over him to hide him anyway that's our family story and on the back of the silver cigarette case is an engraved list of places where my military grandfather served all across the world. And a card of Picasso's single line swirling drawing of a cockerel crowing.

The famous man and I are introduced before he is famous. We are each married. Soon we go to choose him new spectacles. I look at his face in different specs. He likes himself in the specs I like him in. We have lunch each week in a restaurant that has horse meat on the menu that we don't eat. He asks me why I seem afraid. I say I don't know. He asks if I enjoy my work. I say I do but my job has grown such a lot I should be paid more. He says have you asked. I say where d'you think I was brought up of course I haven't asked for more money. He says in this country if you don't ask it will not happen. I say I don't know what to say. He tells me. I go back to my office and say what he said to say to my boss. Straight away my pay is increased.

He says a psychiatrist asked him at their second session how do you feel about me. He tells the psychiatrist I do not come here and pay you to discuss your problems and leaves. I say the psychiatrist was clever he was telling you that you don't need a psychiatrist.

I return to my own country. Our marriages end. He telephones me late at night. He becomes famous. He says write to me it is difficult for you to call me. He asks me what people with power in my country are thinking. I think how unusual for a man to ask questions.

I have a woman friend who will become very famous when she marries her fiancé and I ask her how she will survive all those dinners placed between famous men she's never met and probably won't meet again. She says oh it's quite easy. You sit down at the table. The soup is brought in. You turn to the man on your right. You say do tell me about yourself. He will. The soup plates are taken away and the main course is brought in. You turn to the man on your left. You say do tell me about yourself. He will. The main course is taken away and desert is brought in. You turn back to the man on your right. You say do tell me more about yourself. And he will. We laugh. I don't say rather you than me.

I fly to the famous man's city for my work. We go out to a restaurant. He says he has to leave his laundry at a launderette on the way. I say do you think now you are famous you can get someone to do your laundry. He says you think so. I say I do.

He comes to my country. He stays in a grand hotel. In his room we watch the President the famous man advises on television. I ask are those things he is saying all true. The famous man says he is drunk again and telling lies and he'd told him not to say those things. I say he looks quite gay that way he stands at the podium one foot pointed behind the other like in a ballet pose. The famous man says it is a miracle that man has fathered two children. A line of motorcycle police is parked below his window. Ready to protect the famous man.

We walk in my park. A security man walks behind us with a gun. A neighbour stares. The famous man says I miss you I must start a small war somewhere near to you so that I will see you more. Write to me more often. I enjoy your letters.

The doorman of a strip club entrance below my office grins up at me each evening when I leave work. He says d'ya wanna job love. Even when I have a streaming cold or if it shows that I've been crying. I am much taller than him.

In the country he lives in the famous man invites me to lunch at The Ritz. The maître d'hôtel says we can't come in because my white peep-toe Courrèges ankle boots fashionable in my city are not permitted in The Ritz. The famous man fails to negotiate the maître d'hôtel to allow us to have our lunch in The Ritz. We walk around the corner to a Chinese.

A man at a party tells me he is unhappily obsessively in love with a girl who only meets him for lunch at The Ritz.

The man always books a room hoping that after they've had lunch together he can persuade the girl to make love to him in the room he's booked. I am wondering how many booked rooms stay empty in The Ritz at lunchtime every day and what must I do to get myself into one.

In a country near my country the now very famous man tries to negotiate an end to a foreign war his government is fighting. Some evenings after work I fly to where he is. I meet him in a beautiful house his government have bought from a banking family. The famous man and his negotiating team live in the beautiful house. Negotiations with the enemy team take place in the city suburbs.

I wait for him in the ballroom. All the furniture is underneath white sheets hidden from daytime sun. I get bored waiting. I see myself in ornate gold mirrors dancing past ghostly shapes. The famous man leads me up a staircase. Military police stand to attention on the stairs. He says to one young man she worked for MI5 you think it is safe for me to bring her here. The young man looks anxious. His fingers inside his white glove touch his gun slotted into a white leather holster. Upstairs the war negotiating team sit at an oblong polished mahogany table. Fresh fruit is in a crystal glass bowl. He introduces me and says be very careful what you say the oranges are bugged. His team all laugh at his joke.

I am afraid he can be a cruel man.

We wait inside the front hallway looking out at the cobbled courtyard. I see what seems like a thousand paparazzi sat on motorbikes beyond tall wrought iron gates. Each pillion rider carries a camera with an enormous lense. To shoot photos of the famous man. Fleur-de-lis and coat of arms in the gate's wrought iron designs are pretty. The gates swing open. A car drives out of the courtyard with a man in the back. The man resembles the famous man. A pork pie hat is on the car's back window ledge. The car and the lookalike famous man race off. Paparazzi motorbikes roar after the car. The famous man says I never wear a hat they put it in my car as a decoy. We leave the courtyard in a hatless different car. I hunch low down.

We have dinner at a restaurant at a table at the very back. An empty table for ten is between us and the other diners. Perhaps so the famous man is less likely to be recognised I am thinking. Halfway through our meal I see ten people nearly fall in the restaurant door laughing and talking about a great day at the races. I hear their Irish voices. They order champagne. I see two Irish cousins. They see me. They call out darling what can you be doing here miles from home come and sit with us and bring your little friend. I say hello hello thanks very much but we'll stay where we are. He and I go back to arguing about the morality of his government bombing a nation adjacent to the country that he and his President believe should be defended from a political system they disagree with. I say the bombing is cruel and wrong.

His government's rationale for the war is predicated on honour. A fight to bring democratic government to a faraway country. And the Domino Theory. That their enemy aspires to conquer the free world. Bit by bit. I say to him your family escaped from your childhood country. Escaped a dictator who really was trying to conquer the free world. So of course you fear the same will happen again. That's not so in this war. He tells me about unspeakable cruelties being carried out in the place where his nation is fighting. He says to me so are you saying you want these things to happen. We argue on and on. I am anxious about whether I am a bad person to enjoy being with him. In the war nearly sixty thousand thousand soldiers of his nation's military die. A hundred thousand people are bombed in the adjacent country. The famous man negotiates peace without honour.

He is to travel secretly to a distant country that's been his nation's enemy for a quarter of a century. He hopes to negotiate a potentially internationally celebrated visit by his President. Secret plans are created. At a formal dinner the famous man apologises that he feels unwell. He leaves. His host leaves also to drive the famous man secretly to an airport in the family car. The family car keys cannot be found anywhere. The international secret plan is in jeopardy. There is panic. The keys are found in the teenage son's jacket pocket. The famous man takes a long secret flight alone.

In the distant country the famous man is taken to an empty room. He tells me when the foreign country's delegation team come in each wear identical grey suits white shirts black shoes and carry identical black briefcases. Negotiations through a translator begin. At a point of disagreement the delegation team stand up snap briefcases shut leave the room without explanation or saying if they will return. He feels afraid as he sits on his own. No one from his country knows the exact place he has been taken to. Time passes slowly. He thinks of me. I say did you also say that to your President. The delegation return and negotiations succeed.

In his President's grand formal office the President's dog

chews a rug while they discuss international relations. The President gives the dog a biscuit. The famous man tells the President you are teaching the dog to chew the rug.

The famous man talks with a strong foreign accent. He says his brother who has no foreign accent was asked how come there is such a difference between the way the two of you speak and his brother replied I am the brother who listens.

In my city he asks to come to see me after a formal dinner. My mother and my aunt are staying overnight so as to be close to the airport for their flights abroad next morning. They wait up to meet the famous man. It gets late. They say we can't wait up any longer. They go upstairs and then come back down in nightdresses and quilted dressing gowns and furry slippers. They sit side-by-side on my sofa. He arrives. He tells amusing anecdotes and we all laugh together. The next day he and I go to lunch in a restaurant. He asks why are your aunt and your mother flying to different places in the same country today. I say as a matter of fact they are each going to see their lovers. He says what a family. We both laugh happily.

He asks me to go on holiday with him in a beautiful place I've wanted to go to. I say thank you but I cannot come. I don't tell him why.

– Mouthing –

Each day I long to see Mr St George a short man I met only the once he bent his face close to mine a face I've now made large by my desire for him so many of us desire him in nights and days of pain oh to lie back in his adjustable chair for him to fight tooth dragons it's a fact that right now England wants a hundred a thousand more of our beloved Mr St George.

At my free NHS dentist fish criss-cross a water tank searching gloomily for seas and rivers. The last dentist and his receptionist stole the private patients' money and put it on the horses. The new receptionist sits alone with the fish on Fridays no one knows where the dentist goes.

It's June and last year's root canal has gone bad. Now cardboard X-ray slides dig in my gums the dentist says my pain is a tiny nerve strand says I'll probably have to wait a year for treatment my jaw's on fire my ear heats up I slurp soup and porridge I sigh while June July August September come and go then one October morning a government minister on the radio says . . . there are plenty of NHS dentists in this country enough for everyone for every specialist treatment he actually says if you are sitting at home with toothache waiting for root canal work to be done don't just sit there get up do something.

So up I get bus tube bus to big old Eastman Dental Hospital walk through big old empty rooms on big worn out old carpets past big dark furniture into new open plan area rows of new dental work stations not one person sat at any I arrive at reception four girls in blue-and-white stripes sit at computer screens patients wait in attitudes of pain it's here I came and here I am the morning passes quietly no one screams fourteen of us wait one taps a mobile phone one stares at a wall one lays her head on a partner one reads a paperback one shuts his eyes two small boys kiss.

A nurse says we'll see patients as quickly as we can clinic ends at 1 p.m. high on a wall a TV plays soap operas with subtitles on and on at midday a girl in blue stripes tells me we have no record of you no referral from your dentist you are not known to us and I say so if I'd not come today I'd have waited forever she tap-taps high heels away a hate of government rises in me am I a casualty of the Iraq war governments enjoy war more than dentistry that's for sure the blue striped girl says we will check referrals again.

A girl waiting starts to cry her henna'd hair curls shiver a girl in a pink dress leans on a doorpost eyes closed the four stripy receptionists grumble . . . he does it all the time . . . if he doesn't send us patients' notes what are we supposed to do . . . a man is told to go home and an old lady who shouts to us I'd best go to the toilet first I realise I'll need a new referral and new X-rays I go bus tube bus back to my dentist tell the receptionist my June referral didn't arrive and it's October now my dentist says it's the hospital that's lost your referral lie down I'll take new X-rays I'll write you a new referral are the antibiotics any help no? I'll give you stronger ones I say not penicillin it makes me depressed he says you're getting depressed anyway I can see why he says hospitals grown long backlogs mistakes happen my work isn't per hour that a treatment takes so I refer work unnecessarily to hospitals or I'd work for nothing on the long jobs like root canal instead of doing the work here.

Back to Eastman Hospital bus tube bus it's late afternoon the stripey girls say oh you've come again one says I'll take your new X-rays downstairs in the morning I say can I take them downstairs now she says no that's not the system bus tube bus home.

It's November five months after June I call the Eastman Hospital every day friendly voices say no information till a voice says your new X-rays and referral have disappeared I go bus tube bus to the Eastman I talk to Tom temping dental secretary seconded to Mr St George see Tom sit in front of referrals high piles of files say if only he had a secretarial assistant he could clear his desk say he books in six new referrals a day say each referral needs an appointment referral before a referral to one and only consultant Mr St George hear Tom call the records depot at Iron Mountain tell me my records are found they'll send them over here in the next month.

On Google I learn how to do root canal for myself see adverts for cheap quick dentistry in Budapest I am so tired of pain Tom is leaving the Eastman Hospital says he'll write his successor a note for Mr St George oh Tom I wail my file comes back from Iron Mountain on Tom's last day it's in the post room downstairs Tom will fetch it if he has time.

It's December six months after June my ex-husband asks me what I'd like for Christmas I say a box of chocolates would be nice he says he's making lots of money what would I really like I say root canal he says I can go to his private dentist and he'll pay but I must never tell his wife.

In the private dentist's gleaming room Mozart's *The Marriage of Figaro* plays and roses bloom in china vases. I see a painting and recognise the artist the dentist's brother. I say I once chose one of your brother's pictures and took it home and took it back. I didn't have the money.

It all feels so seductive here. I ask the dentist do any of your patients ever fancy you and he says my assistant Mary best answer that and Mary says well we do actually have two lady patients and he tells me don't leave me alone in the room even for one minute with either of those two.

I say heavens whatever would happen didn't you tell me your diamond drill rotates a thousand times per second. Who'd risk a quick kiss. The dentist says an amazing sentence. He says it's very hard to do good dentistry if some woman has her hand on your thigh. Oh my god I think and see myself laid back mouth stuck wide open cotton wool in my gums and lusting and how really money creates very strange situations. I'm certain no patient ever lusted after my NHS dentist in his grubby room situated at the bottom of a council tower block. Or perhaps they did.

When I was a child riding ponies the grown-ups said if you have an accident and get taken to our local hospital with a broken arm or leg you'll very likely come out dead the treatment going on in that place is that bad so don't fall off your pony. And when I did break a collar bone it was all my fault we were galloping hell for leather on a frosty grass slope and my pony's legs slipped from under him I woke up in hospital certain they'd cut my legs off. I couldn't feel my feet anywhere at all. My mother waiting in a passage heard me screaming. A nurse came and said it's the general anaesthetic they gave you it's always the same when they put you under your limbs swell up you'd think they'd have noticed it happens by now I'll get a razor and we'll cut those nice long leather boots of yours off and the swelling will start to go down.

In the panelled waiting room at the private dentist at my next appointment I start Thomas Hardy's novel *The Mayor of Casterbridge.* A young couple and a baby are out in early evening rain after walking all the day long. The girl is so tired. The man plans to sell her when they get down the hill to where they're going. I put my hand onto the page to stop him and say don't please don't do that to her.

At the vet in America are sick dogs cats birds snakes mice every pet under the sun waiting in wood booths and I hear a dog barking and then a receptionist call out hey mister you can't come in here with no animal you don't have no dog with you I'm calling the police if you don't leave right this minute. I stroke Doggo half spaniel half sheep dog Doggo's far from well and he seems sad does he know we'll soon leave America forever without him. Doggo and I first meet one blowy day on the Harvard campus my toddler son runs in an open front door three dogs run out my small son follows and then a lady appears and I say I'm so sorry my little boy's been in your house you've got lovely dogs the lady says two are ours one's a stray and I've called Animal Rescue they can't catch it now the stray stands close beside me I feel in my pocket hurrah I've got string I lead the stray back to our house a skunk smell comes with us I call the vet say how can I get rid of skunk smell on a dog he says put it in the bath and pour tomato juice then milk all over it from then on every morning I leave Doggo and my little boy with the nuns at nursery school or Doggo lies under my desk at the Kennedy Institute of Politics and Jackie Kennedy and Bobby and Teddy all stroke him Doggo is quite famous around Harvard.

This Kennedy Institute where I work is created after JFK is assassinated so politicians can meet with academics. The Secretary for Defense Robert McNamara's driver nearly runs down a student shouting STOP THE VIETNAM WAR and McNamara is led away through underground sewers. That evening I'm at a private supper where anti-war students harangue McNamara until he holds his shaved bullet head in his hands and starts weeping and in London years later I watch his 'Talking Head' film he says he was asked to be Secretary of Defense because he ran the Ford Motor Company he had organisational expertise and US helicopters were falling out of the sky and crashing because of engineering problems he says if he'd not been the man in power if he'd not made the US military efficient would the Vietnam War have ended sooner would fewer lives have been lost and fewer young American men been injured and I sit in the cinema and think was that evening when angry students made him weep was that the start of these his doubts about was the Vietnam War worth it.

My boss's book called *Presidential Power* is a bestseller and pictures the president sat at his desk in the Oval Office behind piles of files so high the president never gets below fire-fighting to preventative action and the book analyses the unworkability of the presidency.

My boss says he is stopping smoking cigarettes. We both chain smoke. The door between our offices stays open. He says he can't watch me smoke cigarettes if he can't. He says he's got us each a pipe. For a year I tamp down tobacco in my pipe bowl. My thumb stinks. I do it because I enjoy my job. I need my job. I am married to a poet. I suck and complain. People give me pipes. A green pipe a curly pipe a long white pipe. Then we go home to Ireland.

– The Punks Then –

Teenage punks are everywhere. Now four crowd into a small bathroom. Door closes. Nice boys getting clean thinks mum of one. Transformed clean loveable boys. Boys reappear. Four shaved-sides heads four stiff-soaped coxcombs pink turquoise orange purple on crowns of heads down backs of necks to tiny tails. It is hard to love them. Mum of one is scared. For herself. For them. Are punks wanting war with everyone. Big silvery safety pins stuck in noses. Johnny Rotten faces on dirty T-shirts. White muslin nappies pinned over crotches. Punks take drugs she's never heard of. Punk music screams fuck you all. Lyrics she thinks she'll die of boredom listening to. Not any laughter. Not studying working earning boys. All telling lies. It's a terrible time to be a mum. Boys go to prison. Some die. We are political they yell. You are the reason why. Parents rage weep moan. Mothers tell each other we don't know who our boys are. Not any more.

Teenagers she's cooked spaghetti suppers for break in her home. Take a handsaw from a cupboard. Cut a hole in a fridge door. Smash ragged gaps in doors. Write fuck off on walls. Smash picture glass. Burn holes in carpets. She weeps what am I doing wrong. Where is the fun we used to have. Why's family forgotten. What's happening. Where are birthdays Christmases. Where's getting fed up with rainy weather. Where's going to college and work and joining a Trade Union. Fighting for better wages and paid holidays.

Years go by. Only the odd solitary punk now. Mum of one sits in a cafe with a young ex-punk friend. They drink hot chocolate. She listens to his broken heart story. Again. And again. She's bored. She says remember punk clothes your nappy pinned on ripped jeans torn shirt remember my washing machine tore your stuff apart several times and I said sorry the machine's gone wrong well the washing machine was working fine actually I'd turned up the water temperature to max heaviest duty wash and fastest spin so the wash wrecked your stuff. She smiles at him expects him to laugh. He stares at her. He says you lied. You lied to me. She says yes I did and more than once. She's laughing. Happy she did something bad. Not always a victim mother in tears. He says I can't believe what you're telling me. You did that. You lied. She stops her laughter. She says sorry sweetheart I'm so sorry.

The stories mum of one hears in rehab. Crumbs. As we used to say in the pony club when a very big jump happened. A boy in drug rehab's granny dies leaves her fortune to him. Not to mum and dad. Suddenly he is rich. He buys a Jaguar XK150. Thinks what'll I do with the rest. I guess I'll take drugs again. Years go by. He sees old addicts having a bad time. Getting ill. Getting busted. Going to prison. Dying. He books himself into expensive rehab. Calls his parents first time in years. Parents say your grandmother's money should be ours. You get out of that expensive clinic. If you don't we're taking you to court. We'll fight you. You'll see what happens.

A surgeon is in rehab. He's stolen hospital drugs before doing operations. If he can't find enough drugs in the cupboard he blackmails junior surgeons to go out to buy him street drugs. If they refuse they don't get promoted by him. Won't go up the ladder. He says it's a miracle I didn't kill anyone. We the relatives and friends of addicts say it's very likely you did.

County parents join rehab relatives. He's in tweeds she wears pearls. Father says they've heard about an easier rehab treatment that's quicker than months doing the twelve step system a capsule inserted under the skin stops a craving for drugs. A boy in recovery says yes he knows about the capsule treatment. Says his friend had it done. Says it worked fine until it was Easter and his friend wanted to party again with them. Says we had to get the capsule out. Unfortunately the penknife wasn't clean. Says his friend's leg got infected his friend had to go to hospital and have his leg amputated luckily it was below the knee.

In the bad years sometimes I know where the person I love is and I mail postcards sending love. One day I kiss a postcard before I put it in the letterbox. A day later a lady I don't know stops me in a street says I saw you kiss a card before you posted it I just want to say how lovely for you to be having such happiness I wish I was.

I write this at the kitchen table. I see the person I love come up the steps to my front door. We wave and smile at each other through the window. I go and open the door and for the thousandth time I am thinking what someone wrote: Surely of all the wonders of the world the horizon is the greatest.

During the addiction years I wrote a story.

In his library Tolly opens the locked cupboard where he keeps Elizabeth's gold cross and his father's pair of engraved guns and The Use of Life by Lubbock his only school prize and a box of Havana cigars given to him by a friend after Elizabeth dies. He cleans both guns pushes oiled swabs up and down barrels as if to strengthen his arm. A cartridge falls off the table. Floss his daughter and her friends scream their song refrain . . . he's a mongoloid a mongoloid says fuck to his parents he's a son of Freud he's a mongoloid. Carefully Tolly writes Dear Dr Vickers I am worried about Floss. She does not eat regularly. Yesterday I asked her to heat a chicken pie for lunch. In the kitchen I found the cooker burning. I put the fire out without difficulty. I am at a loss to know how to care for Floss. Had Elizabeth been here now I believe Floss's life would be different. I hope you can advise me. Yours ever.

Walking to the village he posts the letter then he fetches his gun and waits quietly among elm trees in the sheltered dell for pigeons. But the music sends them veering away from their resting places. In the hallway Tolly reaches up pulls out electrical fuses. Floss leads shambling boys towards him. Their eyes look down to groin level. They offer in monosyllables to mend the electricity. He says the electricity will come on again tomorrow. He smiles broadly at them. He says why don't you go for a walk. Lovely evening. You might gain inspiration. I'm off to bed early. Lots of garden-

ing after church tomorrow. He shifts the gun a little. He thinks Floss looks ill. He remembers her running towards him a year earlier. A boy wheezes. One says what we gonna do. One says I bin keeping back some smack for a little occasion. One says to Floss you fucking said we could play our shit here. They file past Tolly and outside. Tolly sleeps quickly in the wonderful silence the old gun under his bed his small change coins and the electrical fuses on his bedside table. Floss dies leaning against an oak tree. When he finds her the youths have disappeared. Leaving behind their amplifiers that look like black coffins.

It's ice-cold weather. The person I love isn't at the squat he was at. A girl a skeleton in sleeveless black dress pale yellow tangled hair opens the door. She tells me where to go to next to find him. I say thank you so very very much. I place my hand on her shoulder. Her boney bones. I say is there anything I can do for you. She picks my hand off like it's filth turns slams the door. I find the person I love. We drive to rehab as agreed a month ago and at last a bed's available. As I drive I shake the person I love's going rigid body. I say over and over don't die please don't die we'll be there soon. We get there. I ring the bell. A woman opens the door sees figure slumped against me looks back over her shoulder calls get the doctor.

The other day in my kitchen we laugh about that day. Yes. Can you believe that. Wasn't I wearing a girl's pink dress the person I love says. You're a monster I say. We shake with laughter. It's metamorphosis. The miracle. And what I've written in lipstick on my bedroom mirror: The only person I can change is myself the only person I can . . . Then mirror space runs out. The person I love says it's through grace that addicts don't relapse. I say Simone Weil wrote our only expectations of life can come from work and everything over and above is a grace. We talk a lot on nearly every Saturday morning

The person I love has been to many funerals. Lost many friends. Survivors of addiction look out for each other. They mentor addicts who are new to rehab. Addicts come from everywhere. Rich. Poor. Middling. Any culture. Some are friends now over two decades. They come over to celebrate the person I love's twenty years clean birthday. They are friendly. Wise in certain ways. Someone should write a social history of them. If I was young and clever I would.

– Christmas in the Shires –

Coconut knickers he says and quick I am on a beach palm trees bamboo huts roofs made of leaves bare foot boys running along white sand and I look sideways in the backseat of the car there is a man. Drizzle falls from grey clouds on Boxing Day.

In England on Boxing Day for two hundred years fox-hunters have a jamboree that is they ride to an open space in the countryside led by Master and two Huntsmen in red coats called pink by hunting folk that's people who prefer England the way it was before World War 11 better than now I mean they like all the comforts of post-war life but not all these yobbos in anoraks here today. I see a man point say not my sort old boy.

Anyway there I am in light drizzle among the anoraks horses hounds children country friends pissed off families the day after Christmas when their presents didn't work out so well grown-up children arrived late when the turkey has been carved into a tiny mountain of brown things and getting cold and my rellies married and kind give me a big time hello it's good to see you what have you been up to a good bit louder than their other words in case I might say actually I'm only here because it's lonely to stay home alone even though we all can see from a mile off that's what I am so thanks for having me I do appreciate it and when will we have a drink I should really tell you or perhaps better not I shall get through this Christmas by drinking a lot of your whisky and quite a lot of your wine thank you thank you.

There I am in the same old drizzle as the last paragraph on Boxing Day like lots of people are in Hampshire, Leicestershire, Gloucestershire the Shires people who all have bit of a hankering for the past brought on by sentimental depression that comes with too much food and glug glug alcohol to get through Christmas without a cross word there wasn't a cross word people say afterwards as if they've imagined peace and goodwill not remembered Uncle Johnny broke Aunt Cora's jaw on the staircase and Aunt Cora's bony little body flew down the stairs her legs waggling in the air landing on married for the third time host's weeping daughter wailing where is daddy mummy a child who carries two dogs begging fire tongs she won't she absolutely won't leave her house without can you beat it those fire tongs belonged to her bloody father child takes his bloody tongs to school and to damned ballet lessons and out hunting all over the damned place Aunt Cora's flying body lands on or nearly on the child who falls in such a way that tongs swizzle in her little hands and dear brass doggies thump her quite new front teeth and there's blood and tears and a man shouts bloody hell what the fuck's happened now meaning it's always always like this at Christmas.

There I am in the drizzle wanting guess what it is I'm wanting more than anything in the world you'll never guess I want a horse a great big gee-gee a groomed to gleaming led to Boxing Day hunt meet by a groom a horse with swoopy curvy bum a tum stuffed full of oats and bran a jingling ring-ling curb chain on a double-bridle that sings its merry song when horse shakes its head so someone in an anorak or see-through plastic mac will look up really up at me from below my bum say looks like that animal is raring to try to get you off aren't you frightened sitting so high up there on top of him and I say smiling down definitely down at the someone who's ventured out of town into countryside on Boxing Day to have a gander at us someone who never stands to attention while 'God Save the Queen' plays on the family radio on Christmas Day someone who is listening to the fox hunter tribe mutter those yobbos make my blood boil there I'd be up on my horse soon to joggle thrust up down up down in my saddle say steady boy don't want a slip-up remembering my mother's horse rear up off tarmac fall over on its back scrabbling horse legs a lump on the road not moving then moving a little a crying noise and then all the ghastly stuff of pain driving to hospital unconscious conscious her brain might be damaged d'you think oh shut up for god's sake just drive just bloody drive don't talk ok.

Well that won't happen today because my mother sadly is dead and I stand in muddy rellies wellies and yes you guessed it in an anorak not tribal fox hunting plumage a rellie stands right beside me in the drizzle talks in a voice that sounds as if luscious plums roll around his tongue plums voice loud as calling a dog to heel or matron's voice at boarding school where he's spent a lot of time as a boy obeying shouts and bells a voice I wish would talk quieter as if it doesn't want to be overheard in case other people might not see things exactly the same way here I am stood by him I am someone to share things with on Boxing Day. I'm so confused. Their tribal kindness their generosity. But sometimes their superior cruel words.

Like at Christmas Eve supper one rellie denigrates a gay Labour Party Government Minister. I say if I was gay would you have me to stay he says I'd have you to stay but I wouldn't have you in my bedroom I say I wouldn't be in your bedroom for all the tea in China thanks very much. I've been playing with his two small sons maybe he fears his children have been tainted by liberal socialism by playing with me. I say to him let's play a game let's pretend I'm called Fred and you're called Silvie may I have a little more wine please Silvie and miraculously he laughs and we play my game till midnight on Christmas Eve.

– Vienna –

My father says Cockerel shot dead his brother officer Limpet Jackson in the war and my mother says that can't have happened Cockerel wasn't court marshalled for heaven's sake and my father says in all wars confusion reigns no one sees a lot of things that happen Cockerel damned near worshipped Vienna then she went and married bloody Limpet.

Vienna and Cockerel's wedding after wartime is in St James's Piccadilly and I am the smallest bridesmaid and I step carefully behind her exquisite train of hand sewn Irish lace which slides sleepily across flagstones my small satin slippers shine and I am thinking I want to be married just like Vienna especially at the church door as pink rose petals are thrown at us and then I sit in a Rolls Royce between other bridesmaids and in the Dorchester Hotel foyer I spend a penny behind a tree like I do on our farm and my mother arrives and says I'll take you to the Ladies and I say I spent a penny already and she says where and I point at the tree and my mother leans down to whisper in my ear don't tell anyone.

What follows is a story about a schoolboy from another country. Cockerel and Limpet and my father first encounter Ahmed when he arrives at their boarding school and same as all new boys he folds back their sheets polishes their shoes builds miniature coal pyramids in fire grates toasts bread for their tea in the flames fetches their sweets from the school tuck shop runs to place their racing bets in High Street betting shops the same as all new boys have to and older boys short-change him and tell him he can't count English money until they discover that Ahmed's father could buy a hundred times over all the homes and horses their families own.

Back then small boys sent away from home to boarding schools were not told what to expect when they got there certainly not a foreign boy. Ahmed has heard women behind lattice screens whisper insults at Sephardic Jews for using cheap clothes dye by mixing betel nut with rare crimson cork oak sap and he's seen African workers in his own country their wrists tied by ropes as punishment so they cannot reach their bowls of camel milk after they complain the milk tastes of sand and wouldn't be fed to scorpions where they come from. His father would think that for his son to become a servant at school was very wrong.

Older boys in black-and-white checkerboard spongebag trousers starched white collar shirts flower embroidered waistcoats ask Ahmed what's your father's name and when Ahmed replies Emir of the Highest King Abdul al Farah Prince Latif al Said and bows they are so amazed they all guffaw and point at the small boy and say tell us again go on tell us what your daddy's name is again.

Ahmed learns to paint with watercolours and he bicycles out into fields and woods returning with pictures of blue tits thrushes chaffinches wild English birds and in every painting high up in a top corner a hawk hovers preparing to dive for the kill and he daydreams his father's royal hawks fly thousands of miles from desert skies to circle in air thermals high above the lush English countryside. He has the *Racing Post* delivered and studies flat racing and tells any boy who asks him what horse to bet on in which race and the horse he picks usually wins. In his last summer term at boarding school on Derby Day he finds a floorboard in his room pulled up and all his hidden cigarettes made from tobacco grown among almond trees for aroma tipped out on the floor. His black ebony cigarette box the lid decorated with a gold sun in a desert dawn and the cigarettes are stamped into small crushed pieces and tiny brown tobacco worms.

He imagines a grown-up world where he'd lead his own champion racehorses into the winner's enclosure. That actually happens. My father says he's never heard of anything remotely like it when Ahmed's horses win the Derby and the St Leger and the Oaks. And every other damned race worth winning my father says.

My mother and Vienna meet Ahmed at a dance. Ahmed looks exhausted and mistrustful and my mother wants to put her arms around him. Luckily for my existence she is in love with my father and she leaves the party early. Ahmed and Vienna waltz together and dance the foxtrot and he says he will drive her home when the party's over. Vienna waits for him. She asks another girl how long are you staying. The girl says she is waiting for Ahmed. Vienna sees Ahmed still dancing telling a girl something and the girl is saying yes I will.

The next part of the story is so simple and there's no knowing what is true and what Vienna makes up later. She says Ahmed sees her leave and that he follows her taxi in his car and outside the flat she shares with my mother they talk for ages in his car and he asks her for her telephone number. After that he certainly telephones her each day and she is the girl he takes racing and he gives her a diamond hawk with ruby eyes and a white Alvis car after she tells him how she adored her pet white rabbit and he tells her every Alvis car has a silver rabbit mascot on the bonnet. Ahmed says he is very sorry but he cannot invite her out in the evenings.

After Vienna and Cockerel's wedding her love affair with Ahmed begins and before long Vienna is begging Ahmed to take her far away forever to his country or to anywhere. He does not hide their love affair. He sends her bouquets of red roses because she likes his red and green racing colours. Scented mimosa clipped into ebony fingers is in the back of the chauffeured car that fetches her and brings her home next morning to the house in foxhunting country where she and Cockerel live. If Ahmed keeps her waiting she is brought a silver dolphin full of Iranian caviar kept cool in crushed ice and a long handled silver spoon.

Cockerel is so unhappy he often stays at our house. I lean against the bathroom door to hear him pray out loud in the bath. Or he stays out late at his club gambling on cards at chemin de fer. He drinks too many Brandy Alexanders and grows bloated and red veins appear on his face. My mother worries that he whips his dogs and his horses.

Cockerel dies out hunting of a broken neck. And a broken heart. He thunders towards fences as if he lives for those moments in the air when there are no choices about what can happen next. One day his horse rises at a high stone wall and too late Cockerel must have seen a deep narrow tarmac road the other side. The horse's front legs stiff with panic thrust inside the roof of a car. Noises like wartime happen. The driver and his fiancée miraculously live but suffer terrible injuries and sue Cockerel's estate. Ahmed ends their love affair and after paying out compensation and legal fees Vienna has no more money. She sells her diamond hawk with ruby eyes and her white Alvis and she lives with us for the rest of her long life.

Vienna goes steadily deaf. To begin with she says she hears dance music more clearly than talk and she sits in her armchair pointing her black tin hearing trumpet at our wind-up gramophone. She listens to Strauss waltzes and Sounds From The Hunting Field on easy to break shellac records that somehow haven't broken that I listen to now while I write about Vienna. Hounds yowl Master's whip cracks his horn blows Gone Away his voice yells come along all you little bitches now come on along. Vienna heard my mother and my father's deeper voices. She shouted at me I can't hear you child for heaven's sake speak up. So it is for Vienna that I first learn how to write.

– Stow Fair –

A lovely curvy girl gold sequins twink-wink on scarlet nylon tankini top and matching scarlet French knickers red stilettos tap tap tarmac her fake mink coat sweeps road grit in early morning rain. She's on her way to Stow-on-the-Wold Horse Fair. So am I. She looks my way. I say fantastic outfit. She says made it myself it took four months. I say hope the weather improves. A horsebox driver in flat tweed cap shouts spoilt it this weather innit. A girl yells at her mobile phone is that you Wayne listen I'm telling you Wayne you sell any Wayne did you Wayne you're a proper fucker Wayne you listen to me.

In muddy gateway ruts my boots stick and then I'm on a grassy slope among caravans parked beside plastic tables displaying stuff for sale horse shaped glass jars towers of plates dark blue purple gold baby bootees cork bathmats smocked dresses for children bridles martingales saddles chrome stirrup irons crocheted shawls in sunset colours miniature gold slippers men's leather brogues lemon plastic straw parasols dripping rain on cut glass goblets a frog riding a motorbike yells Meet Dangerous Dirk six television screens show the same rippling manes swishing tails skewbald racing trotter a man stands flicks his hazel switch at nettles shouts to me they call that animal Diesel greatest stepper since forever how far d'you go back with Stow Fair then a woman behind the caravan calls is that horse Diesel still alive the man calls back yes love he's in Blackpool last I heard and points at a piebald on the six screens says that one'll make a class stepper by next spring.

I slip and slide wish for a walking stick pass rained on gold dresses garbage bins marked Dior gold necklaces gold earrings a mother I'd seen up the lane calls out doormats six pounds today a young boy sits in a film director chair his jar of pebbles slotted in the arm a plastic pistol in his hand his small dark shades swivel towards a target bang bang bang pebbles fly his father stomach from here to kingdom come cackles you'll never get a bloody bullseye.

Gold is everywhere gold chainmail handbags birdcages gold high heel sandals royal crowns on shoes gold boots hair combs straw hats baby's gold bottles gold dummies photograph frames gold lace frills on tiny dresses to match layettes under gold parasols an Elvis lookalike winks carousel balloon horses fly on strings a handsome boy with black hair combed into a quiff comes up close stares in my eyes says hello it's been a long time you've different clothes on I say you're a lovely boy I walk on in rain pass a gasoline generator four fake marble cherubims Dior lettered cushions two teenage girls viewing sparkling dancing shoes one says there's lovely things for girls isn't there the other says I begged of mum two Irish women talk will you look at that dear Jesus in heaven Lonnie Donegan sings 'The Grand Coolie Dam' a toy carousel twirls porcelain figurines in wide china hats and ball gowns a live ash blonde girl's muddy silver glitter sandals tread a black plastic pistol into the mud her mum in beige hand-knitted cardigan points at a BARE FISTED FIGHT sign says we always used to go to that.

I break off a hazel stick and start downhill a bare chested charioteer stands on a board between two wheels gallops a snow white mare uphill and down a skewbald stallion tethered on a chain paws the ground prances neighs the white mare dashes past him again again tiny Shetlands shelter from wind grey rain clouds race across the sky ponies shake shaggy manes a lady in a tweed jacket calms an Appaloosa steady boy walk nicely the spotted Appaloosa shies at a brass cowboy Dolly Parton sings I fall to pieces gingham layettes swing in the rain I ask a man how much and he weighs a gold necklace says two and a half grams four-fifty I say four hundred and fifty pounds he nods looks me up and down I say it's lovely but I'm not a sale I finger gold spanners on a bracelet. I'm getting cold.

A tannoy yells where the fuck are you now a red car passes close to a piebald's heels the piebald's driver calls whoa-whoa my darling go on get on you cretin horseshoes crack gunfire cracks on tarmac on tv screens lovely particoloured horses stand sleeping a black Fell pony nuzzles my hand I look in his eyes wish him back at home with me whenever my Fell steps a chestnut yearling takes a step police horses stand stock still the RSPCA officer asks mounted police what's going on a police rider looks down says there's things changing hands at five six seven times the price I'd say. I want to take a grey donkey home and my Fell pony and two skewbalds and the prancing piebald stallion and the two police horses. Sounds of ponies neighing rise into the sky higher than human voices ever can.

By the field gate a bonfire burns a terrier tied to green

wheel of old fashioned caravan barks on and on the caravan shafts rest on pink horse heads posts a man argues on a mobile phone two tables right I did I told you yesterday he kicks at a chained brindle lurcher chewing a rope of raw sausages ponies roped to a horse trailer stamp hooves shake forelocks a tattoo on a man's shaved head says FIGHT. I'm tired now and sad. I don't want to watch ponies and horses I'd buy if I didn't live in town sold in Stow Fair auction ring. I want to go home.

– Princess Diana's Funeral –

The night before. Westminster gold stone spires. Strangers who talk.

I brought flowers for her
Have a Mars Bar Jelly Baby sausage biscuit
Where's the nearest toilet
There's one on Westminster Bridge and one more I don't know where
Oh-oh this is my favourite song Jon Bon Jovi *I'll-always-love-ove-you*
They took her body to Kensington Palace
Where's that
Where we took the flowers to remember
Yes
You still wanting to go to the toilet
Shut up
What's that you're saying
They're asking if I'm going to the toilet
What did you say
I said I want to know where to go for the middle of the night
Are you selling those
When I've tied the ribbons can I borrow your torch
What's it for
On Monday I'm doing the London Women's Run I'm

sponsored for breast cancer research
Where are you staying
I'm over there on the corner by the barricades
The Mayor of London's going to the funeral honest
I believe you
We've got a Union Jack we brought one with us
Have you oh well I've got my knickers
Nine o'clock and all's well

On the far side of Parliament Square two yellow cranes high elegant as girls wait by a dark blue sky to dance. Big Ben's clock face stares. Houses of Parliament buildings biscuit stone. The House of Lords fire yellow. St Margaret's Church ash white. Westminster Abbey dark. Buildings behind tall trees. Buildings against a velvet blue sky. Stone frills ruffs crinkles gorgeous as dresses we remember her in. Waiting.

A radio says we'll have clear skies tonight
They let the people follow her into Kensington Palace
Did they
That's okay isn't it
How far is it to the portaloo
Miles
Really
Over Whitehall and down an alley by the pub
Is it mixed
Uh-huh
They're giving away hot food over there
Is it from Harrods
You're a snob
What did she say

She said is the hot food over there from Harrods
You're a cool one aren't you asking that
Look if I put the torch in my mouth you can see right through my cheeks
Creepy
Have some wine
No it's yours
She's drinking it out of a school-lunch thermos
Excuse me excuse me you know that photo you took of the flowers and Big Ben
Yes
Can you send me a copy can I give you my address
Course I'll bring a paper and pen down where you are when you come back
Will you you're such a star

Smiles.

How many girls have you been out with in the last year
I don't know
How many come on
Lizzie mostly
And how many you've pulled
That word pulled it's the worst of your generation's bonking's awful pulling's worse
Sorry I know but
How many have you tongued
Ugh now you've gone too far
Anyone like a free cup of tea we've got one too many
That man he looks cheerful not
Ask him if he's okay

You over there you all right standing up I can tear off a
piece of our plastic for you to sit on
Shhh that's what he came for
He looks all on his own
That's his statement he's making he wants to okay
No it isn't he's security leave him alone stupid

The radio journalist says this is the love zone on London's Number One radio hit Love Station.

D'you really feel she's gone
I do
I don't
It'll hit you in the morning
Look love don't go putting your stuff there it blocks the
way through you'll be moved on you squeeze in here
oh Lord the compromises you make

Eleven o'clock strikes deep as bells under the sea. Burial at sea. Burial on land.

Look at that foreign motor coach coming past wave go
on be sociable Germany from Germany or Hungary
is it
Glad you came
Mmmm really
Wouldn't've missed it for anything
Even though people are talking and radios are playing
it's still sombre isn't it
Yup
Magnificent occasion
Yeah isn't it

Why do I feel it's a long time we've all waited to be
friends not to be scared of you know
I know I don't know
I think the same too
Here are the others coming back just as I was thinking
it's time they reappeared
What's it like up at the portaloos
It's fine only one's working they're cleaning the others
Are there a lot of people
Mmm people're camping out all along Whitehall on the
traffic islands
In between traffic everywhere
It'll be solid up there by morning
First they said four million then they said six now it's
eight
I was up at Buckingham Palace on Thursday putting
some flowers down and I asked a policeman how are
you coping and he said we've had to draft extras in
from all over the country
Anyone for a Pringle
Oh I'll have one now
There's crisps and chicken and jelly babies
And brandy
It's nice where the Cathedral roof's gone blue
Mmm I'm surprised at that part of the Abbey over
there that's so dark they haven't lit it up
Eleven-fifteen there are so many of us
If you lay your flowers down first look go over there
then come back here over where there's that long line
of flowers put yours over there too

Oh all right then
I can see the back of Churchill's statue he's an old
elephant in bronze

This morning June in our hardware shop lent me her shop ladder to bring then I found this plastic stool that's lighter and upside down it turns into a bucket so I took her ladder back to her shop and she said have you got a golf umbrella and I said I have got a brolly it's not a golf and she pulls out a big red candy striped brolly in cellophane paper and says here you are you take this one I've been meaning to put it in my son Graham's car I'll do that with it afterwards I say I s'pose you couldn't come with us and June says I would if I could I did it for Winston. Her husband is upstairs he's on a gas cylinder or else he can't breathe. I've heard him shout at her.

Look at that wispy white cloud it's heart-shaped
There's a silver paper heart and arrow up a tree
Everyone's walking about everyone who's not settled is
looking for a place to stop and rest
Watch those two girls walking down the aisle of flowers
stopping to bend they look lovely
I saw on a telly programme that if police arrest a child
prostitute for soliciting men in cars the police say I'm
arresting you for dipping and peering isn't that weird
See you later have a good day a good night
Look you can just see our policeman his eyebrows are
going up like this look at mine let's call to him Brian-
Brian-Brian

In darkness stone turns gold. How precious our patches of paving are now. Every passer-by wants to sit by us with us under us. Anywhere. Candle-flame lozenge shapes blow back and forth in the breeze. A flag high on a tower loops over over in slow waltz time. A dark-haired girl wears a man's jacket sits up under orange pattern duvet looks around looks at me. We grin.

When you're at Oxford Circus which road do you take do you go downhill I still don't understand
I'm ringing my daddy Daddy Daddy are you asleep can you hear me have you got my doggie good good it's fine here yes okay I'll see you tomorrow
I must be cold because I've got trousers and socks on I did go out once with one pair of socks on and I came back in another pair
I'm going to sleep I'm so tired
Are you
Over that side over there absolutely everyone's asleep everyone
I'll take you for a walk down there there's thousands thousands and thousands
When exactly do they go into the Abbey
When I grow up I want to be a nurse or a teacher or a fireman I can't believe I'm lying on the pavement I've never done anything like this in my whole life
Chocolate biscuit
Chuck it over
Don't throw food
Can't give it away can you nobody likes our food
This is my breakfast

I've got toothbrush and toothpaste
And water
Anybody for an Iceland
What're they like
They're okay they're Icelandish not like Marks and Sparks
No thanks
Chicken leg
They've got the funniest food Mars Bars and chicken legs
And garlic cheese don't forget your garlic cheese we'll all stand close to you you'll scare everyone off with your garlic cheese smell
D'you know the Michael Jackson dick-lick joke why doesn't Michael Jackson put ice-cream on his dick because
That's revolting that's horrible
Mother Teresa died today it says on the radio
Pull the aerial over

Twelve o'clock midnight. We're all so relieved to be together in this great people heap. The cranes are green now. So is the filigree on Big Ben's clock face. That's because the sky has gone black. The breeze seems light off-white. Soda-pop sunrise.

Hello I'm going for a walk down to the Abbey I'm going with them love you
Mmmm
Did you see the flowers at Kensington Palace were there a lot

Yes like by the sea when there's a little bay and as the sun goes down or comes up the sea reflects all the colours in the sky it's waves and waves of colours it's lovely

Really beautiful

What the hell is that will it eat me Stamp on it go on

Don't do that it's a bug it lives here we don't live here it's got a right

Oh look isn't that sweet that man driving his delivery truck handed out a bouquet he did out of his truck window

What are you doing now

I'm wide awake watching that dickhead over there film I'm watching his camera lights

Look it's lovely parliament roof turning blue isn't it I never imagined that happened did you

D'you want a Scotch egg Scotch egg anybody no no yes hooray I can't get rid of Scotch eggs

Look isn't she a darling Where

Over there handing out the Scotch eggs a little Trojan

I've got eight eggs left

Go down to the drunks they'll eat anything but be careful very careful

Do they want any over on the bench

Try the guards see if you can find a handsome one call out catch

She's doing very well she'd make a Good Samaritan

The last Scotch egg the very last one

Give it to that old guy over there with greasy hair

You look comfortable

Thank you I've discovered part of the art of life is
finding how to be comfortable anywhere
I did it all the eggs are gone
Well done one two three for she's a jolly good fellow for
she's a jolly good
Shhh people are asleep
Mother Teresa died today
I know I heard
They'll be together now
With her and him and the driver
And our granny and my dad
And the king
The king I can't even think about the king
When the flag over Buckingham Palace flies on top of
the mast the Queen's at home it's the royal standard
so if a king or queen dies it's there for the next one –
The king is dead long live the king
Anyone want to play snap
We could play cheat
D'you wanna come and play cards with us
Anyone for a game of cards
Strip poker
Are you cold come over here
I know someone who'll be asleep in Barcelona
My first baby who died was called Mona
Anybody want a packet of crisp-bread
Yesss
No no it can't be it can't over there a boy's banging his
forehead on a wall

Suddenly I'm weeping. A radio announces this is the three o'clock news.

Doughnut who wants a doughnut
Over here throw it
Whoops
Yeah over here
We do we do
Whoops it's gone on your front has it have you got it
Mmm yum yum
We're moving quick put our stuff in bags put it in and get the sleeping bags off the ground that's it yes off we go
It's a stampede but where to
Nowhere
Where's our friends
Sit down now quick quickly keep this space
These false nails aren't going to last long you know
Why not
I think I'll put another layer of resin on when I'm home
How long till they open the barriers
How many rows of people are there in front of me
Six it looks like
Traffic's stopped
Eventually we'll be allowed to go as far as the white line in the road
Frank Bruno sent his regards didn't he can't remember what it was he said but it made me smile he's lovely
D'you know what my niece said it was so sad
What
I wish I was dead then I might be liked more she's only

seven I reckon she gets bullied at school
Can you do anything about it
I dunno I remember while I was living with them I used to wake up at night she was crying her eyes out it all went to her nose I had to watch out she was still breathing remember that day I went to pick her up to surprise her I went to school I was waiting then I saw her crying she flung her arms around me saying I've lost my coat don't tell Mum her new one
Look those two're still sleeping his head's on her knees
Get up get up we're on the move again
The barriers aren't moving can't you all have some consideration for the people who've been here a lot longer than you have

We are tired now and getting grumpy.

Things like us playing cards seems like a year ago doesn't it or is it just me thinks that
Sorry sorry toilet
Can't you hold on a minute
There's no room to move
Brandy brandy anyone want brandy or hot coffee here comes the bottle here just hold onto that glass bottle we'll put it in a bin
The policewoman wants some coffee too here it comes hold on to it tight
Thanks thanks appreciation thanks
The darkest hour is just before dawn that's a Mamas and Papas song it's so sad the big one choked
Did she ughhh

You've got to curl up on the floor like everyone else you can't stretch out like that
Tree's gone black
There's conkers on it already
They're not conkers it's a London plane tree their trunks are a flaky mess
There's our policeman leaving hurray whooeee it's a new shift now
Okay back to sleep
You warm enough
Yes
It's no good I've got to get in my sleeping bag it's cold now

It's five to six. Sunrise. We don't look too beautiful. Quiet crinkled dead droopy. Policemen stride past our lumpy bodies. A radio says the orchestral conductor Georg Solti has died he lived down the end of our street. One guy's slept all night his trimmed orange mustachios small plump bird wings his woolly grey blanket pattern yellow leaves his yellow peak cap says Johnnie Walker in green words. A radio says beautiful autumnal morning. More in the way of sunshine. Atmosphere of great good nature. Great sadness. Three lemon cranes are turning grey in white gold dawn. Parliament's blue roof every stone ripple in relief. Every leaf green. Pigeons police creased jeans tangled hair tired eyelids finger knuckles girl spoons sleeping. A red blue white flag above Big Ben.

What's that chopping sawing the screeching noise
They're cutting down traffic lights and lamp posts

they've cut down everything in people's view
Any rubbish any more rubbish pass it over over here
that's it That's all there is

A brown ant stands on top of our white thermos lid. Wiggles its antennae. A soprano sings through static of a tired radio battery. Nessun solo. Nessun solo. The ant runs to the thermos lid edge looks bewildered while the soprano sings. Girls lie on the pavement lovely relaxed as if it's after a night of marvellous love. Two policemen stand at the barrier lips pursed eyes flick over us fast as snakes' eyes. Looking for what looking for danger. The chopping noise goes on. A radio says seen from the sky the sun rising is a great golden ball. The river a silver ribbon. Hyde Park an ocean of tents. A sea of flowers forms an enormous cross by Kensington Palace. Barriers put across Thames bridges. A man mistook flowers for people in Trafalgar Square. He'd seen down from Capital Radio rooftop. Four red balloons float over the Abbey. A leaf falls from the tree onto my head. That's good luck. Seven o'clock in the morning. I pick up my grandfather's copy of *Cranford* a novel I read at school I only remember a cow falls into a lime pit so the cow's hair gets burned off. The Cranford ladies knit the cow a woollen coat. The first line reads In the first place Cranford is in possession of the Amazons. Radio says six million people. She was such a great lady. Our voices murmur except for a drunk shouting at his shaved head son Michael I'm telling you the drunk swings a two-thirds empty white wine bottle you wanna go to the Serpentine and swim do ya well do ya. Some leaves are rust coloured around the rim. Eight o'clock in the morning.

D'you mind if I put my feet on your sleeping bag
I dunno yeah go on
I'm getting knobbly bumps on my bum
Hurray hurray hear that clapping they got the last street lights down
It's quite far to Kensington Palace
We'll go together after

Helicopter blade sounds. Giants whip cream. Tired people's heads loll on shoulders. Bags bottles brollies brothers babies. No no no. No babies here.

Anyone want dark chocolate it's really black and yummy I got it at a boat party last night it didn't cost me a thing I couldn't believe it we went at six-thirty and the party was over by nine o'clock like a kid's party
I'd like a shower
It's like people bought up all the flower shops
Before Queen Victoria died a man bought up all the black velvet in England so then when people were told to wear black he made his fortune
Don't jiggle not only did you wake me up by kicking me now you're making me ruin my eyeliner
I love the things people do with their mouths when they put on their eyeliner
St Margaret's Church spires look like octopuses' knobbly stone legs
Pin on your big Union Jack with your black bow pin it onto your coat so you can pin all the layers together
Yes and pin it to your skin as well then it will be really safe

Whoohoo Geri Spice is on the radio it's party time
What time will we get back to school
Where's school
Burford in the country it took an hour and twenty minutes coming up here by bus
Did the school let you come
No we left a note saying where we'd gone
She'll let us have showers before we go back into lessons won't she
She will not she'll have phoned our parents by now you just wait
Tell you what we've got two and a third more hours so we might as well get our bums down
Yeah I'm not standing for that long

We clap as a truck drives by. High up on a stone pillar in the early sun a boy reads *Hello!* magazine. Our princess is on the front cover in a lovely black velvet dress. A small man walks down the road. He pulls a Council cleaning cart past the Cathedral. He sweeps up horse shit. He shovels turds into a green box on his green cart. A line of people dressed in black queue between us and Westminster Abbey doors. A radio says never before witnessed such friendliness between public and police. A half-muffled tenor bell rings as it will every minute of this journey. Very little to hear. Very little sound. Voices slowly dying away as they realise. A second line of mounted police.

Look there's Will Smith from Men in Black
Where
He's gone round the corner after this blond guy

who looked kind of sinister as if he was somebody important then came Will Smith so the blond guy must've been Will Smith's bodyguard

The barricades get moved. We seem to swim quietly across the road in shoals in front of seaweed trees in dapply light. We watch clerics stand in rows behind Abbey railings in long scarlet robes their scarlet skirts swing a little. Horses' hooves like lots of china cups clatter saucers sounds. A radio says at snail's pace the coffin goes. The first police motorcycle outriders are out of the sunlight. In the life of our country. Draped in the Royal Standard. Royal lilies white roses. Families holding each other quietly. The street cleaner in his fluorescent green passes by pulling his green cart. We loved her perfect complexion. So many of our complexions are imperfect.

They're starting to go into the Abbey
Those boys must be Prince William's and Prince Harry's schoolmates from school
Oh that's good they'll be someone for them to talk to about it
Okay?
Hot
I don't know how to help you
What happens if I fall off this stool
Get down now
I can't really get down there isn't room to stand up

Someone helps her down into the shade. She sits on tarmac hugs her knees. She's wrapped in a Union Jack.

Amazing heat in this sun feel my face. Here comes the green

street cleaner in his fluorescent green jacket with his shovel and brush. No cart. A black plastic bag.

> That lady in a cartwheel black hat she's the daughter of Barbara Cartland who is ninety-something Barbara Cartland wears blue sticky eyelashes out to kingdom come she dictates a romantic novel a month she says six men are in love with her
>
> Policemen are wilting a bit
>
> For really famous people like Elton John and Will Smith and Michael Jackson too if he was here there must be another entrance round the back of the Abbey
>
> They're coming down Whitehall I really can't see I might be able to if some little squirt didn't put her hand over the eyepiece of my periscope

Laughter.

> It'll be nice if we're all a bit more like her after this won't it
>
> Mmmm
>
> Look it's mostly men in our neck of the woods two to one men to women
>
> Loads of toads

A policeman shouts at us you on the left don't move any more to the left there's a danger there are young children there please please all hold your ground the procession will pass by. We hear clapping further up the road by the main door into the Abbey.

> That might be the Queen
>
> They're lucky those people up there they're nearer

We're lucky too we can see a lot down here look back at all those people who can't see a thing

A radio says death is a terrible thing. Dignity. The people's princess now far away. Everyone's turning pink in hot morning Mediterraneanish holiday sun. Somebody's crouched down in shade among legs with a notebook to shade her head.

I wonder if anyone ever stands by railings looking at a policeman for so long that the person and the policeman fall in love
Don't know really have you picked one
No and I don't see one that's picked me either
It's nearly reached us now
Just down there isn't it listen
You can't hear anything except horses' hooves
Is it coming past here
Yup
And back afterwards
Nods

Someone's crying. Nearly everyone's looking in the same direction. Autumn leaves are shaking. The sun's gone in. A Royal Standard rises above Westminster Abbey roof. Clapping ripples. Fast shallow water crosses stones.

Sounds like one carriage wheel needs oil doesn't it
Look at the security guys on the Cathedral roof
They're here they're here
Is she in there

We're very quiet as she passes. A few people weep. Horses walk slow. Soldiers' black fur Busbies hide her coffin. A bugle blows. Three notes. Three times. A bell tolls. Charity workers wear wide white sashes. Guardsmen's gold tassels on red coats. Music. Happy and glorious. Long to reign over us. A choir sings. Gorgeous music plays from loudspeakers in trees. Prayers.

. . . the secrets of our hearts . . . merciful . . . oh holy and most merciful . . . oh lay lu . . . amen . . . amen . . . again amen . . . her loving family . . . commanded the sympathy of millions . . . her life and enjoyment of it . . . I vow to thee my country all earthly things above

A horse whinnies a high anxious descending scale.

. . . we pray for . . . our grateful hearts . . . and soul by soul and silently the shining bands increase . . . at peace

In the trees a soprano sings. A young man in green sweater green baseball cap leans against the trunk of a London plane his fingers poised delicate as beautiful insects. A Cabbage White butterfly pirouettes overhead flies on up Victoria Street towards Westminster Abbey main door.

. . . time is too slow for . . . too swift for those who fear . . . too long for those who grieve . . . too short for those who love . . . but for those who are gone . . . time is eternity . . . shepherd . . . forever . . . thy rod and staff . . . endless days

Bright clouds turn the Royal Standard flag gauzy.

. . . though I speak with the tongues of angels and have not love . . . prophecy . . . knowledge . . . faith . . . all my goodness . . . my body . . . and have not love . . . I am nothing . . . love is . . . rejoiceth in the faith . . . believeth . . . hopeth

. . . endureth . . . never faileth . . . when I was a child . . . when I became a man . . . I put away childish things . . . now I see through a glass darkly . . . but then face to face . . . then I shall know as I am known

The policewoman holds back her tears. I am crying. A pretty forty-year-old brunette is crying. A tall sixty-year-old man is crying. Everyone is crying. We all sing.

. . . it seems to me you've lived your life like a candle in the wind . . . if your footsteps will always fall . . . in England's greenest hills . . . your candle burnt out long before your legend ever will . . . goodbye England's rose

Every one of us outside cheers Elton John. A dog starts barking.

. . . again we say . . . we give thanks . . . Lord . . . hear our prayers . . . Lord of the Suffering . . . hear our prayers . . . hope faith love . . . the greatest of these is love . . . I would be true . . . I would be strong . . . I would be brave . . . let us join one and other . . . Our Father who art in heaven

The choir is quiet. I listen to hoof beats in the sky far away. It must be drums or the Cathedral organ. Two boys in black turbans cling by fingertips onto a branch. Silence. Red balloon hearts float up over trees. Pull red ribbons into blue sky. Red hearts fly miles into clouds. One heart circles Big Ben. Here she comes past us again. We're all clapping.

Would you like a little water
Is that it
Yes

– C.R.A.F.T. –

Oh god a woman says to her friend in the street I've forgotten something senior moment another one and it's only going to get worse. Her friend says not a senior moment C.R.A.F.T. What's C.R.A.F.T. says first friend? Second friend says Can't Remember A Fucking Thing.

They laugh two ladies in the leafy summer street their cotton flowered skirts shake their eyes shine.

Three days later well two or three or four or five or some days later the friends meet in the street again. First friend says what was that thing you told me the other day about not remembering? Second friend says that's funny very funny. She laughs and her flowery cotton skirt shakes and her eyes shine. But the first friend says no I really can't remember. Second friend stops laughing and says C.R.A.F.T. Can't Remember A Fucking Thing. They stand still and look into each other's eyes and soon soon one or the other feels afraid it may be her next not the other or it will be both. Then who will help and how lonely will it be not to remember who each other is. They turn to walk back up the summer street and their flowery cotton skirts swing gently and they go indoors.

―Acknowledgements―

With huge thanks to Rosalind Porter my publisher at Notting Hill Editions

Margaret Halton my Agent at PEW Literary Agency

Matthew Burne for designing my book cover

Ali Smith & Sarah Wood at Esolo Unorso for publishing *Strangers Who Talk*

Cesca Echlin for early re-typing & editing

Jen Tuckey for art

Willie Rearden for horses & genetics & gardens

Heathcote Ruthven & Roo, Juno, Nell & Jed Nimmo, my grandchildren, for their stories

And Fanny Howe, my American poet friend, who I wish was still in this world